PRAISE FOR
DARK, DIRTY, DANGEROUS

In more than 20 years covering the stories of business owners for *Inc.* magazine, *Forbes*, the *New York Times*, and now *21 Hats*, I've come across few stories as moving and instructive as the story of what Karla Trotman has accomplished with Electro Soft. From figuring out that she actually did want to join the family business to taking part in today's manufacturing revolution, Karla's journey is relevant especially to manufacturers and underrepresented entrepreneurs but really to everyone building a business.

— **Loren Feldman,**
Founder, 21 Hats Media

Karla Trotman is a force to be reckoned with! Her provocative and practical insights about how to create more opportunity for a diverse workforce and revitalize manufacturing have been a long time coming. From how to attract a younger, more diverse talent pool, to building strategic partnerships to being a woman of color in a male-dominated industry, she covers a lot of ground. Sharing her experiences and her revelations in a direct, no-nonsense style, *Dark, Dirty, Dangerous* is an eye-opening and engaging must-read for every leader who wants to make a difference in the world.

— **Cheryl Beth Kuchler,**
Founder and President, CEO Think Tank

Dark, Dirty, Dangerous serves as a timely thought-piece that pulls the reader deeper into a story filled with relevance and prescience. Karla's journey is told through the eyes of Woman in a profoundly male-dominated sector. This book is a must-read for all CEOs and aspiring corporate leaders in this increasingly diverse country called America that still struggles to embrace diversity and its value.

In the intricate landscape of electronic components manufacturing, there emerges a figure whose impact transcends the circuits and soldering joints. Karla Trotman, a visionary entrepreneur and the driving force behind Electro Soft, has not only revolutionized the industry through her very presence but has etched her name in the realm of transformative leadership.

As the pages of her journey unfold, one witnesses a narrative of resilience, innovation, and a relentless pursuit of excellence. Karla's journey as a woman owner in a traditionally male-dominated field is nothing short of necessary and inspirational. She dismantles stereotypes, shatters glass ceilings, and paves the way for a generation of women aspiring to conquer the realms of science and technology.

At the core of Electro Soft's ongoing success lies Karla's unwavering commitment, as a second-generation owner, to innovation and growth. Karla also commits herself to ongoing personal and professional development in fashion rare amongst corporate leaders. Her keen business acumen, willingness to collaborate with peers and mentees alike, and dedication to delivering cutting-edge products have positioned the company for exponential growth.

What sets Karla apart extends beyond the confines of the manufacturing floor. She has cultivated a corporate culture that values diversity, fosters innovation, and champions sustainability. Electro Soft embodies a community where individuals are empowered to contribute their uniqueness and perspectives, driving the company's innovation engine.

As the pages turn, the narrative expands to Karla's philanthropic endeavors. Her commitment to diversity and representation exists in her efforts that reach beyond profit margins. From supporting STEM workforce development to championing supplier diversity, Karla exemplifies a holistic approach to business—one that embraces its role as a catalyst for positive change.

In the tapestry of leadership, Karla stands as a luminary, casting a radiant light on what is possible when brilliance, courage, and compassion converge. Her story is a beacon for those navigating unwelcoming waters, charted expertly by Karla to create routes to success. It lies as testament to the fact that only Karla can define the heights she can reach.

To close, Karla's narrative is a source of inspiration, innovation, and impact. Her journey with Electro Soft is not just a success story; it is a tome of the transformative power of Black women in leadership, and it leaves an indelible mark on the landscape of manufacturing.

— Brian K. Oglesby,
President/CEO, Eastern Minority Supplier Development Council

DARK,
DIRTY,
DANGEROUS

KARLA TROTMAN

DARK, DIRTY, DANGEROUS

BUILDING

THE VIBRANT FUTURE
OF MANUFACTURING

Advantage | Books

Published by Advantage Books, Charleston, South Carolina.
An imprint of Advantage Media.

ADVANTAGE is a registered trademark, and the Advantage colophon is a trademark of Advantage Media Group, Inc.

Printed in the United States of America.

10 9 8 7 6 5 4 3 2 1

ISBN: 978-1-64225-990-2 (Paperback)
ISBN: 978-1-64225-989-6 (eBook)

Library of Congress Control Number: 2024913166

Cover design by Matthew Morse.
Layout design by Ruthie Wood.

This publication is designed to provide accurate and authoritative information in regard to the subject matter covered. It is sold with the understanding that the publisher is not engaged in rendering legal, accounting, or other professional services. If legal advice or other expert assistance is required, the services of a competent professional person should be sought.

Advantage Books is an imprint of Advantage Media Group. Advantage Media helps busy entrepreneurs, CEOs, and leaders write and publish a book to grow their business and become the authority in their field. Advantage authors comprise an exclusive community of industry professionals, idea-makers, and thought leaders. For more information go to **advantagemedia.com**.

To my mother. Your sacrifice changed the trajectory of our family. Thank you for your strength and resolve to keep going.

CONTENTS

ACKNOWLEDGMENTS

There is no doubt that the blessings received by my entire family are the product of praying grandmothers. With that, I'd like to first and foremost thank God for hearing their prayers, allowing our family to become successful in the world of manufacturing.

Thank you to my grandmothers, Shirley Burton Scott and Blanche Wallace, for giving me the most amazing and intelligent parents a child could ever hope for.

To my mother, the most voracious reader I know, I wish you'd had a chance to read this book before leaving us. It is because of you that we were able to still provide for the family while Dad built the company.

Dad, much appreciation to you for building "the company." Thank you for teaching us about business and being an example of what it means to bet on oneself.

To my husband, Thane, thank you for supporting me throughout this journey, from my first midlife crisis to my third. From wanting a career change to going back to school and taking over the family business, I know I'm a lot.

Dylan and Bryce, what an amazing time to be alive for the pair of you. Like Pop Pop did for me, I'm giving you the world as your oyster, allowing you to choose what it is you want out of life. But remember all that I taught you about assets and legacy so that you will have the ability to have your grandchildren eat from what your grandparents created.

To my brothers, TJ and Dan, I love you guys, always.

To the Electro Soft staff, past and present, thank you for being cherished members of the extended Wallace family.

I owe a debt of gratitude to my board of advisors, who "beat me up" on a quarterly basis. You have conditioned me to become a better business owner over these past years, and I appreciate everything you have done for both me and Electro Soft.

Lynnette René Doby, thank you for using your incredible gifts to help me craft this book. It would have taken me eighty-seven years to come up with the right words and phrases that would expertly explain all the information that lives in these pages. You have become such a trusted friend over these past several months. Don't be surprised if I continue calling you!

Lauren Steffes, you poor soul. You had no idea what you were walking into when you got assigned me. Thank you for truly hearing me and helping me get over the finish line. You really did lean in with kindness and care once I told you how the book evolved from simply a manufacturing book to one about my family, the wealth gap, and more. Simply put, I appreciate you.

Matthew Morse, you are a talented graphic designer who really took the time to listen and understand what I envisioned for the cover. Thank you for that.

To Cheryl Beth Kuchler and the CEO Think Tank family, thank you for helping me get through some really rough patches with the business and family. Special thanks to Alix James and Michael K.

Pearson who introduced me to the group. Without our community, I feel like I would be in a padded room, rocking back and forth.

To the Ernst & Young Entrepreneurs Access Network family, thank you for showing me what Electro Soft could be. Without the "access" you have given me, I wouldn't have known the possibilities, nor would I have recast my goals toward "private plane money."

Finally, thank you to the following sources of inspiration and support in both my business and book journey—Sheila Johnson, Sam Johnson, Lee Henderson, Nit Reeder, Kristina de los Angeles Hunter, Phyllis Newhouse, Erica Armstrong Dunbar, Nicole Black, Marcus Lewis, Jessica Johnson Cope, Terry Siman, Patty Angelozzi, Jeremy Ben-zev, and Paul Conway.

INTRODUCTION

To be honest, I never wanted to work in manufacturing.

Manufacturing was a constant in my life as a kid. It was like background scenery—not something I saw myself ever actually doing or taking seriously as a career. When you're younger, you don't realize how much your environment shapes your future. There I was, a Black girl growing up in Montgomery County, Pennsylvania, being raised by college-educated parents who dared to take a risk by starting a Black-owned business.

But it wasn't just any business. It was Electro Soft, a business created in an industry—manufacturing—where, at the time, 6 percent of the population of manufacturing business owners looked like them.[1] This was doubly impressive because Black-owned businesses in the United States circa 1986–1987 were slim, accounting for a mere 3 percent of all US businesses operating at that time.[2] To put it into perspective with more updated stats, in 2020 Black businesses with employed staff made up 2 percent of the business landscape,

1   Thomas D. Boston. "Trends in Minority-Owned Businesses," *America Becoming: Racial Trends and Their Consequences: Volume II.* National Academies Press, accessed May 28, 2024. https://nap.nationalacademies.org/read/9719/chapter/10.

2   Sam Fulwood, III. "Trend/Black Entrepreneurs: Business Owners Narrow Gap with Majority-Owned Firms," accessed October 18, 2023, https://www.latimes.com/archives/la-xpm-1990-09-18-mn-599-story.html.

and the percentage of Black business ownership in manufacturing had only slightly doubled to 11 percent.[3,4] The amount of insight and courage that took inspires me to this day. And I believe the same energy and passion that drove them to keep going are also within me.

Still, I didn't want any part of manufacturing. Or at least that's what I thought. What was I going to do in an industry that, at the time, I thought was dark, dirty, and unappealing? I saw myself with more of a "professional" job. I wanted to be like the businesswomen I saw on TV, and in my mind, the two images did not connect.

I worked in the family business from childhood through high school. When it was time to go to college, my father killed my dreams of becoming a dancer, rationalizing that I was an expensive human who was used to nice things. It was then that I had to decide whether to choose a major aligned with the family business or something else. It wasn't a hard decision. I thought being an engineer was the only path I could take to get into the industry—and I *knew* that wasn't going to happen. Even though I did fairly well in the business competitions and summer programs I participated in at high school, I wasn't interested in any of the business majors most colleges offered.

Fortunately, Penn State offered a "new" major—business logistics. I was familiar with military logistics due to the logistics strategy implemented in the Desert Storm war and because of my father. So, business logistics was a natural choice for me. I finished my coursework, graduated, and went to work in corporate America. And that is when my perspective changed.

---

3   Andre M. Perry, Manann Donoghoe, and Hannah Stephens. "Who Is Driving Black Business Growth? Insights from the Latest Data on Black-Owned Businesses," accessed October 18, 2023, https://www.brookings.edu/articles/who-is-driving-black-business-growth-insights-from-the-latest-data-on-black-owned-businesses/.

4   "Manufacturer Demographics and Statistics in the US," Zippia the Career Expert, accessed September 25, 2023, https://www.zippia.com/manufacturer-jobs/demographics/.

It occurred to me that I didn't really care to work for other people. My degree gave me a different point of view. Logistics is a field of study that focuses on moving product from the point of origin to the point of consumption, no matter what it is. Its goal-centric scope intrigued me. Very quickly I was able to move past the so-called glamour of the career I imagined and found satisfaction in reaching goals logistically. As the years progressed, I continued to change, as did my vision for my future. I had gotten married and had children, so *legacy* was a new word that entered my mind. Eventually, I began to wonder why I didn't put my time and effort into my family's business instead—and *build*. I could put my effort into something substantial: building equity and creating legacy. Working for other people does not allow that privilege.

Business ownership was the bridge that brought me to the realization of what I had, of where I wanted to be, and it allowed me to begin entertaining the idea of running the company. Postcollege, outside the job I had been working, I'd started my own business. I had an online store where I sold products for women who were experiencing discomfort during pregnancy. Building that business showed me how to create value, and I loved how it felt. There is a certain amount of pride in putting in your own time and energy, making your own decisions, and enjoying your own results without having to have constant "meeting about the meeting" meetings and other corporate aggravations. Seeing your ideas come alive and grow into something that held value was nothing like what I experienced in corporate America—and that value was equity.

I knew from then on that I could never achieve that level of fulfillment working for another large company. I decided that day that I, Karla Trotman, the daughter who'd wanted no part of manufacturing, would take over the family business.

In terms of experience, it was a simple transition. The principles and the knowledge I'd gained from the business logistics coursework translated well into manufacturing. Thus, my interest in business helped me see manufacturing in a completely different light. I headed back to school to get my master's degree in business administration and began my journey with my family-owned business.

Getting an executive MBA allowed me to grow in my personal development as a businessperson. To be clear, an MBA doesn't teach students how to run a business. It teaches them to think differently and successfully find solutions for different scenarios in the corporate landscape.

Suddenly, I was interested in things that hadn't necessarily piqued my interest in the past. Ever evolving with new and different initiatives, manufacturing has always been about innovation. What I once found dull and unglamorous, I began to see as exciting and full of potential: it was a brand-new world for me. And while this book is about manufacturing, it's more than just that. It's about how leading with what interests you can unexpectedly take you on a path of doing what you love.

Another goal of this book is to push against the stereotypical thought people hold about the transfer of power in a family business. There is a romanticized fantasy of the parent passing the torch to one of their children: as they run off with it, the parent stands there watching with a tear in their eye. The reality is far more complex than that.

A transference of business ownership can affect personal matters within the family and can cause friction. It's real. I'll share the experience my family and I had in the hope of helping other families to prioritize family-owned businesses transitioning effectively. I want to explain how it's an investment tool. This book is also for the kids of business owners who, like me, felt that working for the family business was not for them. I want them to realize that if they find their footing within the company, they can create equity and something meaningful for themselves and generations to come.

Also, this book is for anyone in the younger generation who is striving to find their footing in the world. Look, I get it. After graduation, it might not be clear which direction to take. I want to reach those students who feel that continuing their education in college isn't for them and help them realize there is another opportunity out there. It's been projected by industry insiders that the next generation of manufacturers will be young people of color and immigrants. If this is you, get ready to find your place in this booming industry.

Within the pages of this book, companies who outsource labor for their projects to other countries may realize there are perfectly capable manufacturers right here on US soil, dedicated to helping them achieve their business standards. So, corporations, I didn't forget about you; I wrote this for you, too.

Lastly, I'm writing this for every Black woman in America aspiring to be a CEO and business owner who knows the odds stacked against us but pushes through anyway, going for what she wants. There are a few Black voices in various barrier industries, which may surprise you, but we're here. I'm here. Your voice can be heard, and you can change the narrative by being yourself and thriving. It's important to me that you hear from me.

Overall, whoever picks up this book, I hope you discover that manufacturing just might surprise you. For example, despite popular belief, yes, you can have a college education or a GED and work in manufacturing. There are many facets and paths you can take.

Within the journey of this book, I'll share with you the wins and challenges of being the president and CEO of a company I watched my parents build brick by brick or circuit board by circuit board. We'll engage in a written dialogue of answers to questions I get asked so frequently that I had to make them into a book for as many people to access as possible.

We'll chat about how to see the things that are not readily on the surface, how to modernize a company in an industry people sleep on, what it means to be a woman in a male-dominated field, actionable steps on how to access capital and financing, effective business strategies, optimal customer service tactics, forming strategic noncompetitive industry partnerships, and more. When you close this book, I hope you realize the possibility of building a very tangible vision for your life.

CHAPTER ONE

How Do We Build a Modern Manufacturing Company?

Manufacturing needs a makeover.

—Karla Trotman, CEO of Electro Soft

Although manufacturing is one of the timeless staples of our society, **manufacturing is not sexy.** It caused a dichotomy shift with its industrialized inception. Our nation would not be what or where it is without it. So, to be clear, it deserves to be held in high esteem. But still, even with all that it's done and where it's brought the nation, it's still not sexy. Not even a little bit.

I realized this firsthand growing up in Pennsylvania with a front-row seat watching my dad, with the support of my mother, build our family company, Electro Soft. I remember seeing him at the kitchen table with a colleague busily working over a pile of multicolored wires. I wasn't quite sure what they were doing, but as I watched them, I knew they were creating something. What I didn't realize at that moment was that my dad was doing more than assembling wires; he was building a legacy. The modest team of two at the kitchen table grew to two more, then to three more, to eventually a full staff. The kitchen table stopped being the main workspace and was replaced by a larger building. Simultaneous with the growth, the company graduated from an idea to a reality. Although this journey was impressive to watch, I still cannot build a case for manufacturing being sexy.

Ironically, as I write this book as the current CEO of the fully actualized and contemporary version of Electro Soft, which celebrated its thirty-seventh year of business in November 2023, I consider the evolution of my perception. I know my definition of manufacturing was shaped primarily by only what I saw on the surface. A cool thing about being a kid of business owners was that I started working at a very young age.

As a child, I was obsessed with earning money. I would rarely turn down the opportunity to take on an odd job. In the early years of Electro Soft, the accommodations weren't so great. I remember sitting at a workbench in the garage with the door open, getting paid twenty-five cents an hour to use a ruler to measure and cut wire for various projects.

Our first leased space wasn't any better. In those early years, one of the company's first buildings had been an automobile repair shop. I would again sit on a bench and get paid twenty-five cents an hour to use a ruler to measure and cut wire to the appropriate lengths for various projects. Grease and oil stains were everywhere. Worst of all, it was hot—no air-conditioning. It was then that I realized I didn't want to suffer in those kinds of working conditions. I didn't understand the magnitude manufacturing held, nor was I trying to.

My early thoughts on manufacturing were a mere fraction of the hub of progression the industry truly is. To me manufacturing was "dark, dirty, and dangerous." There wasn't much excitement, no cute office, which means I couldn't dress well. But most of all, you don't make a lot of money, and I wanted to make a lot of money. I had no idea about the industry's creation quotient. I mean this in terms of innovation, reliable jobs for people, and more. The electronics manufacturing sector alone generates an average of $1.8 trillion in sales.[5]

Manufacturing as a whole plays a vital role in society. If I was unaware of its assets growing up in the industry, imagine how people who don't have any proximity at all to manufacturing see it. This is the crux of the problem. The challenge is changing the perception of the masses so they will get invested in the modernization and evolution of the manufacturing industry. For manufacturing to evolve and simultaneously build successful modernized manufacturing companies, it is crucial to have, among other things but primarily, a sustainable, youthful, and engaged workforce. To do this, there are a couple of factors that need to be brought up to date.

I aim to share with you some concrete factors to consider in establishing a modernized manufacturing company to sustain a thriving and stable manufacturing industrial presence.

In the pages ahead, we'll have a painless historical contextual overview of manufacturing's impact on the US and examine where the industry is now and where it can potentially go. Not to seem cliché, but the old saying is true: those who do not acknowledge the past are doomed to repeat it. Briefly, we'll touch on the innovative minds that are necessary to get us there, and we'll explore them in greater detail later in the book. Trust this. Getting a portion of Generation Z *and* their parents on board is going to take some work. But it's possible.

---

5   "Key Facts and Trends in the US Electronic and Electrical Equipment Manufacturing Industry," IndustrySelect.com, accessed October 17, 2023, https://www.industryse-lect.com/blog/key-facts-on-us-electronics-manufacturing.

Understanding How We Got Here

Industrial manufacturing is the backbone of this country. The Industrial Revolution of the eighteenth century saw our nation reaching new possibilities of mass production, cemented the United States as a chief producer of goods, and placed it at the forefront of technology.

Industrial visionaries such as Andrew Carnegie and John D. Rockefeller and inventors such as George Washington Carver and Alexander Graham Bell shaped our nation's manufacturing landscape. A by-product of this movement was the jobs industrialization provided for US citizens and immigrants, contributing to the diverse fabric of our nation and the formation of the working class. The postrevolution era saw the nation adjusting to support its growth, with labor protection for workers through the creation of unions and the transition of a rural society to a more urban landscape.

Again, the manufacturing industry was the driving factor. This foundational landmark occurrence had a vast impact on present civilization. Additionally, a well-deserved mention is the opportunity manufacturing gave Black American survivors and descendants of chattel slavery. Post slavery, emancipation, the Reconstruction era, and the Civil War, they migrated to the northeastern United States with the hope of societal advancement. They found manufacturing opportunities in towns with booming industrial factories. From there, they were able to establish the beginnings of financial structure.

Today, it seems manufacturing's popularity has been publicly sideswiped by its first cousin, technology. Again, we look to history and see how it happened initially and how modern society is repeating it. In 1946, the first general-purpose computer was invented, followed by computer-aided design software in 1953.[6,7]

With those inventions, digital technology took off and stole the nation's interest and attention, with anticipation of its latest developments, leaving manufacturing relegated to certain industrial enclaves in the US. Our society feels manufacturing's impact more often than it sees it. The early 2000s saw people lined up in front of Apple stores for the latest Apple iPhone release, yet they didn't line up in anticipation for the chips production installed in those phones on the assembly line. Manufacturing is the glue. It upholds the nation by generating vital assets for the Department of Defense's many branches of the military. It supports businesses in the private sector at scale, pushing them toward engineering innovation.

Internally, labor conditions in manufacturing have improved as well. During the Industrial Revolution, workers faced many challenges that no longer exist. Presently there aren't long, grueling hours and unsafe work conditions, and no one is trudging home after work dejectedly with an aluminum lunch pail under a dark and gloomy skyline. Manufacturing just isn't that anymore. Also, diversity has entered the workforce. As a woman in this industry, I know it still has a very long way to go, but there has been slight progress. It's very different today from the environment I experienced when I was younger. This is not my dad's or granddad's manufacturing. I want us to throw open our doors and let people take a good look at what we are and how we do what we do.

---

6   Erica K. Brockmeier, "The World's First General Purpose Computer Turns 75," Penn Today - University of Pennsylvania, accessed September 20, 2023, https://penntoday. upenn.edu/news/worlds-first-general-purpose-computer-turns-75.

7   Adam Robinson, "A Brief History of the American Manufacturing Industry + Infographic," accessed September 25, 2023, https://www.rodongroup.com/ blog/a-brief-history-of-the-american-manufacturing-industry-infographic.

Manufacturing today is undergoing a revolution. It's time to erase the antiquated perception and create a new one. It's time for a shift.

Shifting the Perception: Creating a Renaissance of Revitalization

It's safe to say that if the average person were to think about manufacturing based on their background and limited interaction with this vital industry, any number of images could come to mind. The mention of the word *manufacturing* may produce a mental image of men in sweat-stained uniforms working on an assembly line covered in soot. Again, not sexy.

Consequently, there aren't many eager grads emerging from their educational institutions with the burning desire to have careers in manufacturing. This needs to change.

The future of a modern manufacturing company lies in ensuring that the workforce is replenished with new, young, fresh talent. A shift is necessary to alter how society at large views the industry. Manufacturing needs a makeover, or better yet, a revitalized renaissance.

Again, let's use manufacturing's more enticing first cousin, the tech industry, as a case study. The revamped technology industry has social media and major sexiness on its side. Log into any social media network, and you'll see video clips of influencers jet-setting to tropical destinations with their laptops in tow, coding for three hours beside a beach with crisp, sparkling water.

When I was in high school, the image of a software programmer was a nerdy white guy named Ted, who sported a pocket protector, wore a short-sleeved button-down shirt, and had awkward social skills.

Fast-forward to today. The technology industry is now singularly called "tech," and computer programmers are known simply as "coders." Then, to elevate the status level, add in countless coding boot camps and organizations led by celebrities and media personalities. Their involvement helps make careers in science, technology, engineering, and mathematics (STEM) be seen as solidified, credible, exciting, and pursuable careers.

Now, that's how you reshape an industry—by utilizing the two "*A's*"—accessibility and appeal.

I believe when cultivating and developing a modern version of manufacturing, it's important to change the narrative and perception of how it's seen societally. Manufacturing's public relations need an overhaul to appeal to younger, promising talent. I know it's possible to achieve because I experienced it personally.

Picture this: it was the 1980s, and on TV I saw what I wanted to be—the "working girl."

This archetype in entertainment and media was personified with fabulous characters like Clair Huxtable from *The Cosby Show* and Julia Sugarbaker from *Designing Women*.

That is what I wanted—the romanticized version of what having a job was like. The amazing outfits, the pearls, and the briefcases. I saw myself in nice clothes, taking the train to an office every day. That was totally different from the actual work I did when I was younger, when I spent my days making minimum wage putting labels on the wire I cut, populating printed circuit boards on production lines, and learning how to read prints so we could make products. We made stuff and sat very quietly while doing it. I didn't see the excitement at all. So, when I graduated from college, that vision stayed in my mind. I had no desire to work for my family's business.

Another big part of it, too, was that I didn't get to see the end result. I didn't know what the products were going into. For example, I knew some of them were going into a fighter jet, but I never saw the actual fighter jet. We just made the products and sent them off. Some of them went into check-cashing machines, and I had never even been to a check-cashing place a day in my life. (Note that I am "checking" my privilege. Check cashing and payday loan organizations are a necessity for many unbanked Americans.) Then there were the wires—a bunch of different-colored wires that we were putting together and green circuit boards with parts. I didn't see the impact manufacturing had on the world. I was too far from the outcome of knowing what my efforts produced.

That is, until I saw behind the exterior of manufacturing. I experienced the exclusivity of being behind the scenes and seeing innovation happen months, sometimes years before the public saw it. I began to see the trends of cutting-edge technology and automation by working on the structural components of agricultural robotics and more. Add in the power and organizational aspects of business, equity, and ownership, and I was on board. What changed was that I could see myself in the business.

That's what we must show to the next generation of future manufacturing workers and C-suite executives: the possibilities. Engage them by allowing them to explore. Just about every professional role they can imagine can be incorporated into manufacturing. There truly is a place for everyone. Some people have careers as technicians; there are those with an understanding of assembly. Others are equipped with a knowledge of electricity, an understanding of how currents work, and how to troubleshoot projects. Most of all, people in manufacturing have a natural curiosity. They like to put things together or take them apart and are interested in seeing things built to completion. Commonly, manufacturing professionals like to work independently toward a collective goal. There are a lot of people in this world who enjoy these elements of work.

Unfortunately, they will never learn these opportunities exist without exposure.

Next, if they learn that their interests exist within the industry, then they can see themselves in those roles. Yearly at Electro Soft, we strive to reframe the narrative by joining in a national effort to expose the world to manufacturing. This collective open house effort is called Manufacturing Day. On this one day, manufacturers open their doors, hold tours, and highlight the manufacturing work that is being done here in the US. We aim to change the negative perspectives behind manufacturing.

Although a lot of times solicitors attend wanting to sell to us, we've learned to target our approach by focusing our invites on students, showing them the different side of manufacturing. They typically enjoy the visit, go home, and excitedly share their interest with their parents—then the spark ignited in them is dimmed. The issue then becomes changing the perception of the parents, which is nearly impossible. Parents typically still hold the belief that we've always learned for years: if you want to have a good, strong future, you must go to college. Often, however, the roles I'm recruiting for are floor labor positions. A good fit is maybe someone who did not go to college and who likes to put things together and take them apart.

As of today, the education system does not really bridge that gap, and parents are not wanting to hear their children consider this career path. There is a solution that takes an internal industry effort. As a co-chair of the Southeastern Pennsylvania Manufacturing Alliance (SEPMA), I along with fellow manufacturing leaders have tried to change the outdated perception of manufacturing. Over the years we have created a skills pathway, developed a training program for adults looking to switch into manufacturing careers, and worked with local and state government to emphasize the need for manufacturing workers. SEPMA hired Drexel University's Solutions Institute to do a study to help us understand whom we should be targeting, as our previous hiring methods had proven to be unsuccessful over the years. Collaboratively, we are trying to uncover the cause of not being able to find the people we need to recruit for various roles within our industry.

So far, Drexel has reported that the next generation of manufacturers will include people of color, diverse communities, women, and immigrants. In terms of education, this worker profile may include people who, after one year, decided school is not for them or those with no plans to go to college. In chapter 6, we'll look at how to engage and recruit new talent for the labor work market and other aspects, but for now I'll say that modernizing manufacturing is going to take reframing the industry in students' eyes so they can see themselves in the environment.

Define What Your Modern Manufacturing Company Sells

We've built a successful manufacturing company on a firm foundation by realizing what we sell. Up to this point, you've heard me talk about the projects that my company, Electro Soft, works on. So, you may think you have a general idea of what we sell—printed circuit boards, cables, and enclosures. The actual answer may surprise you.

We sell time and expertise. That's how it's been since the beginning with us. We may have moved from the kitchen table, and I may have upgraded my skill set from wire cutter to CEO, but our intention has always been the same: to provide time-saving, high-quality solutions for our clients. They chose us because we can build what they need, using their specifications and our expertise. We buy the project materials needed to complete the project, and we build the assembly based on the customer's blueprint and bill of material. All assemblies are built to industry standards, on which we pay for everyone on our team to be certified.

Our future workforce will be not only trained in these standards but also under the care of a workforce with years of experience. Everything we make is quality-checked and tested (if the client requests it). Then we ship it to them just as if we were a part of their supply chain. At Electro Soft, we internally frame who we are, and it is present in everything we do. We define who we are for our clients and their outsourced manufacturing arm. Therefore, what we sell is a service, like a consultant or project manager. Think of it this way: a construction company doesn't sell buildings; it sells the time and expertise to build the building.

I urge manufacturing companies to explore what their value proposition is. Ours is embedded in the quality assurance we give to our clients. When a prospective client comes to us, we know they want a couple of things from us. They believe we can build their project and that the price we've quoted is based on our level of expertise and performance, and they know how quickly we can get it done. We then give the client a firm, fixed price to complete the assemblies, and it allows us to gain profit. You can see how we are in the business our service creates.

Now, I'm not implying that we hit the mark 100 percent of the time, because we are human. But when we don't, we go back to the client with the same authenticity and transparency we used to get their business, admit our mistake, and adjust the outcome. It all comes back to how we view ourselves and our presentation as a manufacturing company.

We can position ourselves as more than wire cutters and circuit board makers. Often we make the near impossible possible by taking on complicated contracts with tight turnarounds. We thrive under those circumstances. Our clients trust our experience and level of quality more than they trust it being done in-house. They have told us this on countless occasions. That is why they need us, and the existence of modern manufacturing lies within us and the quality of what we do.

Doing What We Do Responsibly

Another responsibility a modern manufacturer has is its dedication to environmental sustainability. I will say this: Electro Soft does its best to reduce our utilization of lead. It's a well-concerted effort, as lead is an ingredient that is prevalent in production materials. Global government regulations are set in place to lower the use of lead and increase lead-free assembly production. The production volume of lead from mines has decreased from 369 metric tons to 280 metric tons in 2022.[8]

Based on this evidence, the government's regulatory practices are making a dent in lead usage, but there is more progress to be made. In Europe and some other overseas countries, there are restrictions against products manufactured with lead, and it is mandatory that every part of the manufacturing process be lead-free.

So as manufacturers in general, we try to look at ways to minimize environmental impact, like using water-soluble flux during the soldering process. Also, we recycle our cable and solder dross instead of having it hauled away. We also reuse corrugated and shipping

---

8   "Production Volume of Lead from Mines in the United States from 2010 to 2022," Zippia the Career Expert, accessed September 25, 2023, https://www.statista.com/statistics/892365/lead-production-volume-united-states/.

materials. We adhere to every aspect of the process as much as we can and strive to be as Earth-friendly as possible.

The truth is, electronics manufacturing is not a very clean process. We do our best to do every environmentally sound practice that we can do. Every action, no matter how small it is perceived, can help. For instance, major pieces of equipment we have, like reflow ovens, we don't use every day, only on certain days. So, the impact of energy is fairly low.

I'd also add that in addition to environmental responsibility, it's important to consider social governance. In that way, from a social perspective, we are balanced fifty-fifty with male and female employees. We pride ourselves on being extremely diverse. I don't know any other company that is as diverse as we are, starting with me. A Black woman, owner, boss. Diverse. Add to that the four languages that are spoken on our production floor. From a social perspective, we are very much in the community, giving of our time and energy and resources, opening our doors and speaking.

From a governance perspective, we take great pride in running a financially sound company with outside expertise. We have an actual board of diverse advisors that I put together when I took over the company. The board ensures that we govern ourselves as an organization in a solid, sustainable way that helps keep our customers having faith in our continuing.

A modern manufacturing company that operates in excellence and upholds its standards is how we will attract the eyes of those who may have overlooked us. It's how we will pique the interest of a brand-new burgeoning labor market, one unlike we've ever seen. Authenticity, diversity, and unwavering responsibility are how you build, sustain, and evolve a modern manufacturing company.

Reflection Points

• **How do you think about your career? Specifically, regardless of the industry you choose, how do you think about what you want to pursue and do in life?**

Ask yourself, "What were those little nuggets when I was young that got me to the position I'm in or the work that I do? How has it impacted my life?" No matter what type of work you do, *you* are the common factor, and your experiences shape whichever direction you choose. You have the choice to improve it or stay stuck.

• **Manufacturing is not what you think it is. It's so much more.**

I encourage you to be interested in knowing and exploring more. I've been in this industry for years and will never stop learning about it. At the heart of evolution is continuous curiosity. Keep asking the questions to find the impact of what you're making or doing. Learn the ins and outs of the industry. It's all about exploring the curiosity. Reshape the impression you have of this industry, and it may surprise you.

• **What impact do you want to make on those who interact with you in business?**

Evaluate what you are really selling to them. Is it just the surface product, or are you selling more? Once you understand what you are selling, you can form a plan for how to sell it. This one minor shift of understanding will transform your marketing, overall operations, and more. I encourage you to go as deep as you can on this. You may be shocked at what you find, and this change in perception will take your business to a new level.

• **There is beauty in seeing yourself organically in either the family business or your business.**

My family randomly started a business that is still thriving, even though the children of the family didn't want to go into it. My parents never forced us to do it because they wanted us to choose our own future. That could be, in part, why ownership remains within the family. They allowed my interest to grow organically. I grew to see through their efforts that it's possible to change the trajectory of your family through small business ownership. It can be the one thing that begins the cycle of generational wealth. The family business is a vital part of our existence. I can't wait to share what I've learned about the importance, beauty, and challenge of the ever-evolving family business structure.

CHAPTER TWO

Preserving and Reinvigorating a Family Business

Stay far from timid, only make moves when your heart's in it, and live the phrase, "sky's the limit."

—The Notorious B.I.G.

The reality of who I am can be very complex at times. Especially when I share with people that I'm the CEO of my family business. In response, the listener tends to tilt their heads and say to me, "Oh … so, your family gave you a company."

Wrong.

Nothing could be further from the truth. As a reminder, I had a whole job and career that I left behind to pour my skills and talents into the family business. Also, I worked alongside my father during his eleven-year journey to retirement—a journey that was originally supposed to take three years. What people don't realize on the surface is how much I contributed and invested during that transition. First, there was the financial contribution. I leveraged the strength of my assets and credit to take out a huge loan to pay my dad off. I also had to convince bankers and lawyers that I was competent enough to run the company. My story of obtaining ownership is not a feel-good Hallmark holiday movie where my father smiled and opened his hands to take a dollar from me in exchange for the company. No, there was a process of actually compensating him as the founder and current CEO; drawing up legal paperwork with two sets of lawyers, a banker, a financial advisory team, and a CPA; and months of negotiation before we legally transitioned ownership.

This chapter aims to debunk the myths of what it means to take over a family business and to give a blueprint for others aspiring to do the same thing. Also, I want to get into why the institution of the family business is worth the challenge of sustaining. When prioritized, a family business can create amazing, potentially life-changing opportunities. Among them are generational wealth, financial stability, and many more benefits. The family business is the link to a future of financial sustainability and a way to close the ever-widening wealth gap.

Another misconception, adding to the complexity, is that once you do transition ownership of the family business, everyone else involved—staff, family members, and other business associates—fall right in line with the change and welcome you with open arms.

That's not quite how it happens.

It takes a bit of adjustment for everyone to get on board, and it's up to you, the person stepping into power, to set the tone. I found myself telling people that if they were expecting me to be my father, but in a dress, they were going to be disappointed. I remember an instance when a vendor emailed me after he set up a meeting with the purchasing department and asked if we could meet afterward.

Typically, it's hard for me to find a free moment in the day to follow up on emails let alone commit to a last-minute meeting. It wasn't looking likely. Then the vendor mentioned in the email that he always took a brief meeting with my father when he was CEO.

That is one guaranteed way to get me not to do something—telling me what my dad would have done. I'm not my father. My response to him was no response. It was as if the vendor was trying to pull my card, and I reversed it on him. I've found as I transitioned to CEO, several people have attempted to do that to me. It's not a problem; I correct that really quickly by standing in my power (I'll go into that more in chapter 3). I make it clear.

Although my dad and I have both had a hand in operating the same business, we are two different leaders in two vastly different times. His operational practices will not be the same as mine. What *is* the same is the upholding of the principles the business was founded on—making an impression in the marketplace and taking care of our workforce.

As the new owner, it was my priority to take the onus of developing and shaping the company so that it could continue to thrive. To accomplish this, I had to realize the gravity of continuing a family business by taking an honest look into the societal power of the family business, the inner dynamic of my relationship with my family members during the business transition, and the reality of the transference of ownership, then extricate my personal beliefs from the truth.

The Important and Overshadowed Entity: The Black-Owned Family Business

Just as manufacturing is often overlooked for sexier industries, the same thing happens to family businesses. Namely, the tech start-up is a way sexier and more intriguing origin story than a family business. The tech stories are somewhat typical at this point. There is a kid at a prestigious Ivy League university creating his company, living on a diet of "noodles in a cup" and sports drinks. He's so engaged and involved in his start-up that he sleeps on the floor of his workspace and wears the same T-shirt, hoodie, joggers, and torn-up sneakers every day.

Of course, the media eats this up and can't get enough of this emerging "enigmatic," "brilliant," seemingly overnight success story. This newly hatched tech mastermind entrepreneur then goes on to become a highly booked podcast guest and graces the covers of the hottest contemporary media and magazines. He stays hot until the next big thing comes around, and the cycle begins again.

Family businesses, however … not so much. The irony is that family businesses were quite instrumental in forming our society. To be clear, some family businesses do have notoriety. From a historical standpoint, enterprising families that are well known and celebrated, like the Rockefellers, Vanderbilts, DuPonts, and Waltons, are in the annals of established businesses. But their mention in this category is skewed, as they represent only a tiny percentage of the many family-owned businesses in the United States. We only hear about these large companies. There isn't much media attention paid to smaller family businesses.

Specifically, little to no attention or mention is bestowed upon thriving Black family businesses. These businesses deserve to be known for the odds they defy. Despite the obstacles Black-owned businesses experience societally and financially, we persevere. So much so that our businesses thrive, which enables us to hire people from the community, helping them make a living to provide for their families. What we do is truly extraordinary, and it's never painted that way. Little recognition is given to the contributions we make to the national economy, our communities, and our employees. And it's not as if we don't exist; there are numerous Black-owned family businesses, and our stories just aren't told.

There is one family that, due to its historical context, deserves its flowers for its unbelievable story: one of progress, longevity, and determination. With an origin dating to before the Civil War and official incorporation in the 1920s, the McKissack professional design and construction firm is still thriving, yet they are unknown to many. The pioneering patriarch of the McKissack family, Moses McKissack, an enslaved African, reached American soil in 1790 and learned the skill of brickmaking by working for his master, John McKissack.[9] After gaining his freedom, he taught the craft to his son, who had a successful career and passed what he knew to his son. His son, Moses II, along with his brother, Calvin, became licensed architects, the first Black men in the southeastern United States to hold that distinction, and began their family business in 1922.[10]

The two were legends in their field, among the first to initiate a design-build—essentially a concept meaning they would draw a

---

9   Katherine Flynn, "Pioneering Architects: The McKissack Family," The American Institute of Architects, accessed November 12, 2023, https://classic.aia.org/articles/6424065-pioneering-architects-the-mckissack-family.

10   Flynn, "Pioneering Architects: The McKissack Family."

design and then build it.[11] Pouring back into their community, the designing brothers built several of the buildings on the campuses of historically Black colleges and universities (HBCUs) and the library at Tennessee State University; they held legendary distinctions like being the first Black company awarded a multimillion-dollar government contract to build the training grounds for the Tuskegee airmen.[12] From the family lineage of excellence, running the family business now is Cheryl McKissack Daniel. Her sister, Deryl, started her own general contracting firm, McKissack & McKissack, leveraging the family name but financing the start-up on her own.[13,14] One man's commitment to his craft paved the way for not only his immediate family but for future generations.

> I became aware of the McKissack family in 2022 when Deryl and I were both highlighted in *Family Business Magazine* as Transformational Women in Family Business. I was embarrassed that her name, her family's name, was not part of my Black history education.

In 2022, according to the National Council of Architectural Registration Boards (NCARB), Black Americans made up 2 percent of the workforce, with less than six hundred being women. This family

---

11   Flynn, "Pioneering Architects: The McKissack Family."

12   Flynn, "Pioneering Architects: The McKissack Family."

13   Flynn, "Pioneering Architects: The McKissack Family."

14   Samar Khoury, "Separate, But Together: Twin Sisters Break Ground in Construction Industry." *Black EOE Journal*, accessed May 28, 2024, https://mckissack.com/wp-content/uploads/2022/12/McKissack-Article1.pdf.

deserves as much attention as the Ford family and others.[15,16] With a lack of diversity among business holders in the 1920s, we can only imagine what Moses II and his brother endured being the trailblazers they were. That is the legacy and honor of being a Black-owned business. It's about realizing that you can do it a different way. We don't have to be cogs in the corporate machine. We can create a thriving business on our terms. It's an honor to stand on the shoulders of the Black business innovators who came before us. Keeping entrepreneurship alive within our families is a major contribution to closing the wealth gap.

The McKissack family is not alone in its distinction of being a generational Black family that has achieved success. Many legacies exist but are unknown. Stories of successful Black family-owned firms have not been newsworthy. During a prestigious conference, I recently met a man whose family is, as my favorite podcaster, Demetria L. Lucas, would say, "of good coin."[17] They have amassed generational wealth in the truest sense. Anytime you own a private jet and have a family office, you have reached the next level of wealth.

If you're not familiar with the family office structure, here is the technical definition: investment funds that manage the financial assets of the family[18]—that is, when a family business is so big and there's money in other investments across other industries and entities that,

---

15 Milbrandt Architects, "Black History Month: Tackling Racism through Architecture," accessed May 28, 2024, https://www.milbrandtarch.com/2023/02/10/black-history-month-tackling-racism-through-architecture/#:~:text=Nicholson%20writes%20a%20beautiful%20piece,of%20every%205%20black%20architects.

16 Vanessa Romo, "Very Few Architects Are Black. This Woman Is Pushing to Change That," NPR.com, accessed May 28, 2204, https://www.npr.org/2023/03/12/1160836191/black-african-american-architects-architecture.

17 Demetria L. Lucas. Rachet & Respectable, accessed April 2, 2024, https://www.iheart.com/podcast/867-ratchet-respectable-30425527/.

18 Greg Barasia, CFA, "All in the Family—A Guide to Family Offices," Toptal.com, accessed November 15, 2023, https://www.toptal.com/finance/private-equity-consultants/family-office.

instead of retaining a lawyer or accountant, the family hires full-time professionals to service and support the business. There's also a CEO charged with monitoring the family business's operations. Oh, and in case you're wondering if your family business qualifies to reach this level of economic distinction, the lead qualifier is a $100 million-net-worth threshold.[19]

The sad truth is, though, that many Black-owned businesses do not make it because they fail at the point of succession. Either there is no interest from the children in sustaining the company or they don't have the infrastructure or ability to undergo the transition. In general, as a community, Black individuals aren't as likely to engage in a family business ownership transition. Since most Black businesses don't succeed or they fail, they get to the point where they haven't prepared for the next generation.

There is limited data on the breakdown of business transitions of power in Black family-owned businesses, but a study done by the University of California, Santa Cruz, states that 1.4 percent of firms are inherited in the Black community versus 1.7 percent in the white community.[20] Typically, when children are raised by self-employed parents, that is an indicator that they are more likely to be self-employed too.[21] However, based on the small number of inherited businesses and using a little deductive reasoning, something else is contributing to the scarcity of inherited firms. That's why I was

---

19   Barasia, "All in the Family—A Guide to Family Offices."

20   Robert W. Farlie and Alicia M. Robb, "Why Are Black-Owned Businesses Less Successful than White-Owned Businesses? The Role of Families, Inheritance, and Business Human Capital," *Journal of Labor Economics*, Vol. 25, No. 2 (April 2007): p. 296, https://www.jstor.org/stable/10.1086/510763.

21   Robert W. Farlie and Alicia M. Robb, "Why Are Black-Owned Businesses Less Successful Than White-Owned Businesses? The Role of Families, Inheritance, and Business Human Capital."

intent on taking over Electro Soft regardless of the arduous process that was ahead.

The Reality of the Transference of Power

Now that I've established how unique successful Black-owned family businesses are in our society and the Black community, I want to talk about why Black family businesses don't make it from one generation to the next. It's all about the details of the process of succession—passing ownership to subsequent family members. Many families are unprepared and don't know what succession entails, which disrupts the process and sometimes stops it completely. In the next few pages, I'm going to share with you how my family did it. It isn't a beautiful story—it's complex and real. I made significant sacrifices, and the succession shifted our family dynamic. If you're a successor or soon to be facing this transition with your family, you may find value in this section. Your situation may be slightly different, so above all, do what works best for you.

The transition of Electro Soft from my dad to me took eleven years. It was a process. My dad said, "I'm retiring in three years." So, three years came and went, and he said three years again. All things being equal, those three years repeated themselves nearly four times. It dragged along with me in tow. The process began with me being under false pretenses. I always thought it was going to go faster. I mean, the man said he was going to retire! However, I realized I had to take certain steps for him to move forward. It wasn't that he woke up one day, had an epiphany, and said, "I dub thee CEO!" I learned I had to be strategic.

I participated in a training program for companies learning how to pitch for capital called Inner City Capital Connection. Jack Mitchell, of the multigenerational family business Mitchell Stores, was the keynote speaker. During his talk, Mr. Mitchell mentioned the process of having "family meetings." I had never heard of utilizing a family meeting in the succession planning process. Quite honestly, I had never met anyone who had a generational business before either.

Being the voracious reader that I am, I dived into the book Jack Mitchell gifted to us, which was his book *Hug Your Customers: The Proven Way to Personalize Sales and Achieve Astounding Results*. In it, he explains in detail the process and reasoning behind holding family board meetings.[22] I thought it was a brilliant way to keep us all on the same page, because we all had different ideas as to what this transition would look like, who would take the lead, and how to execute the process. So, I initiated family meetings immediately.

The meetings consisted of me, my mother (who was retired), my father, and my two brothers. I took the lead, mandating that these meetings were necessary so that there was clarity as to how the business would transition. We talked about where my brothers and I were in terms of readiness to take over the business. My parents knew my answers, but at the boardroom table, it was the opportunity to understand where each of us was in respect to assets, credit, educational direction, and overall aspirations.

Discussing these details was important because my parents' original rule mandated that no one could participate in the running of the family business until they had obtained a college degree. I felt as if the rule was being unfairly bent for my brothers, who had not completed their schooling. The family meetings allowed us to talk

---

22   Jack Mitchell, *Hug Your Customers: The Proven Way to Personalize Sales and Achieve Astounding Results* (New York: Hachette Books, 2003).

through real-life business and life decisions to chart a path to the next phase. Our conversations allowed us to understand how decisions we made could affect the company and how to do what was needed to protect it.

For instance, all of us were required to have prenuptial agreements in place prior to marriage. Talk about uncomfortable! But that was the mandate to protect the company. Imagine getting a divorce and having to deal with your sibling's ex-spouse. Or worse, your sibling passes away, and the spouse remarries and has a child with someone else, which runs the risk of the business ownership passing to another bloodline. What protections have we put in place to guard against that? Obviously, there are various legal tools that could be put in place, but for us, the first step was the prenup.

Discussing these scenarios allowed us to understand why certain decisions had to be made up front. These meetings were vital, in my opinion, because my parents had in their minds that my brothers and I would equally inherit and run the business. But very quickly I saw what each of us was willing and able to do. It would be extremely inequitable. The questions my parents asked in these meetings highlighted the fact that my brothers weren't on top of some important factors. I can imagine that from a parental perspective it might be difficult to judge your children, but in this instance, it's vital. As a parent, the vision in your mind must be realistic and fair to the child who is willing and able to execute. If these considerations aren't weighed logically, a parent could force a situation that could be destructive to the business—and to the family.

For me, on the other hand, it was obvious in which direction we needed to go. But I knew my parents had to weigh the reality of the situation. Considering going into a potential partnership with my brothers made me pause. When they asked me how I felt about my brothers' future roles in the ownership of the business, I had to tell them honestly. My father told me long ago, "People don't go into business with people who have nothing to offer." In this case, I had finished both my undergraduate and graduate degrees, I had my prenup in place, owned homes and other assets, had corporate experience, and had run my own e-commerce business for eight years.

While my brothers had experience across different industries, none was to the depth and breadth of what I had accomplished. Advisors and banks ask very specific questions about assets and business experience. I was the only one out of the three of us who could cleanly get past the scrutiny. Having to leverage their assets and credit would have increased the cost of capital, thus eating away at our gross margin. All the decisions we had made as individuals up until that point were on display. Plus, we all had eleven years of my father oscillating in his decision.

During that time, I had chosen to go back to school to obtain an MBA because I was serious about getting Electro Soft to the next level. Still, my parents wanted all three of us to take over because they said it would be unfair for one of us to solely inherit an entire business. In my mind's eye, their version of fairness was extremely unfair to me. I'd felt this way for a while, but I wanted my parents to see it too.

It wasn't because I don't love my brothers. I do, but the transition of ownership of a company isn't about love and emotions. It's about business. So, I treated them as business partners. I gave them the same level of scrutiny I would give any other prospective business partner. During our meetings, I also found out that they weren't really into the business. It was more of a sense of duty for them, which I'd also felt at one point in my life but had grown past. I had to face the truth that I didn't want to drag them along.

I made sure to communicate this to them in love. This situation had a certain level of difficulty for me because I had to discover how to balance what was right for the business and at the same time what was right for me. I had to ask myself honestly, "How can I make it so that I am happy—and make the situation effective for Electro Soft?" The hard truth I came to internalize was that I knew I would never be happy working with them if they weren't prepared or engaged.

While these meetings were happening, on the more operational side of the business, I started revamping Electro Soft's entire marketing strategy. At the time, the sales process had shifted, causing us to alter our sales outreach efforts. No longer could you simply walk into a building and take a meeting with a buyer. Friendly waiting rooms were replaced with a simple landline phone and instructions on how to reach the person you were there to visit. We needed another way to break through, so I took the lessons I'd learned with my e-commerce site and shifted them to the Electro Soft website.

Specifically, I began homing in on search engine optimization (SEO), which was relatively new at the time in the industrial sector. Plus, I was doing a lot of management and ownership work while searching for other opportunities and looking for business targets to acquire. As I was doing all this, my brothers weren't around full time. I fully felt the burden of having done everything I was supposed to do to meet the criteria for taking over. They had not. I saw that the bar was being lowered for them by my parents. And I sensed that the expectation was that I would carry them.

I got to the point where I expressed to my parents, "You want me to put forth my assets, credit, experience, and time, then write a check over to my brothers for 66 percent of the proceeds. How is that fair?" I started to really weigh how much time and energy I was pouring into Electro Soft and what I had given up over the years.

The succession plan was stalled, and I felt stuck. So, I started to look around for options, because at the very least, I knew I was bankable.

I weighed my options and one day said to my father, "If you're not ready to transition this company, that is fine. Let me go now. I could work for someone else because other companies are looking for people like me to take over so that they can retire. They'll give me an equity stake, and I can be *their* retirement plan."

I further explained that I was over forty, a minority, and considered in a "protected class."[23] Thankfully I looked younger than I was, because statistically it is harder for protected classes to get jobs because it's difficult to replace us. I felt the need to walk away from Electro Soft and the succession indecision. There are two lessons I want to impart when involved in this phase: don't be afraid to stand your ground, and don't be afraid to walk away.

It's a commonly known rule in the art of negotiation. If you aren't willing and ready to walk away from the table, you truly aren't negotiating. Just because you're dealing with family does not negate this classic rule. Keep that in mind. But you have to be comfortable with your choice. At that time, I felt so defeated that I was willing to walk away from Electro Soft altogether.

Another thing I noticed during the succession was the toll it was taking on my interpersonal relationships. This whole task was beginning to affect the interactions and overall relationship with my family. Everything was taking so long, and we were not living at the means we could have been living at if I were working somewhere else. I had taken a lesser role with a lower salary during the succession. It

---

23 US Equal Opportunity Commission. "Who Is Protected From Employment Discrimination?" accessed March 28, 2024, https://www.eeoc.gov/employers/small-business/3-who-protected-employment-discrimination.

was a part of the personal investment I made into Electro Soft, and I had to see it through. It was stressful, because I was all in.

Simultaneously, I watched friends live the highlife! They were buying their dream homes, taking amazing vacations, and doing life on a different level. It stung a bit knowing my family and I would be living that way, too, if I was working somewhere else. It was a very frustrating period in our lives. For my family's sake, I was steadily pushing my dad to make a decision, and my dad was pushing me back. I found myself stuck in limbo. For a second, I began to wonder if it was possible to have a thriving family life, and take on this business at the same time. It was very difficult and extremely stressful, and I questioned if we'd make it through to the completion.

Then there was this tension between my brothers and me because I felt like they didn't want the company as badly as I wanted it. That made our family "stuff" get into our work "stuff." Things got convoluted at times, and it was a lot! And who could I turn to with these issues without sounding like a spoiled child? Imagine me calling a friend and complaining about how my dad wouldn't hurry up and turn over his company. Who would understand?

When we got to this point, I knew we needed to pivot. So, I called in reinforcements. We needed a third party to sift through all this or else we ran the risk of being stuck. I knew just the entity to help get us on track. When I was in high school, I was in a business competition for entrepreneurs, and one of the coordinators was Terry Simon, the owner of a fee-for-service financial planning office. At that time, my early inner CEO began putting together the pieces in my mind.

I said to myself, "It makes sense for a businessperson to have a financial advisor beholden to them." The entrepreneur would pay the advisor as a service provider, limiting his ability to sell certain products and funds to them. The financial planner would not be incentivized in any other way but to have a fiduciary duty over the concerns of their client's desire to meet their overall financial goals. At that young age, that made a big impression on me. I told myself that one day I was going to be able to afford this guy to take over my finances. So, it only made sense that I reached out to him.

To make the situation even more serendipitous, I'd just read, and fallen in love with, Paul Sullivan's *The Thin Green Line*, and one of the people highlighted in the book was Joe Duran, owner of United Capital. So, at the time I reached out to Terry, ironically, United Capital had acquired his company, and he was the managing director of United Capital's Philadelphia office, which was located a half mile from my house. I wrote him a letter reintroducing myself and reminding him of the context in which we'd met, and I asked if his team helped families' transitions. He stated they did. It was all aligned. I explained the situation to Terry and told him he needed to speak to my father. Then I invited both Terry and the team to Electro Soft.

I picked Terry because I knew he could go toe to toe with my father. I think one of the biggest elements that can impede progress as companies transition power is that the family member who was in charge is used to being the boss. You need an experienced, impartial party who can counter them and any defenses they have. Choose wisely. If you bring in the wrong person, they'll be walked all over. I knew that Terry had enough experience and success, and more importantly, I felt he wanted to help me. When my father saw Terry's cost, or any cost for that matter, like most small business owners would, he said, "Forget it." I met with other transition advisors, but I fought for Terry and his team, and they were worth the battle. Besides, some of the other companies I was prospecting would not have worked. I knew within one conversation that my dad would have walked all over them. Terry was the best fit, and he did right by us.

The first thing Terry and his team did was to have someone perform an impartial evaluation and interview my brothers and me. They then shared with my parents verifiable data showing which child should be running the company. They pointed out how each of my brothers had aspirations, but these weren't to run the family business. It made sense, because in one of our family board meetings, I asked my brothers what happiness looked like to them.

One of my brothers said he wanted a large acreage of land to build a farm and live off it. Mind you, he had no farming experience. My father explained to him that farming is very difficult. My other brother wasn't clear on what happiness looked like for him. He is an artistic soul who happens to also be brilliant with computers. For him, Electro Soft was more of a duty as opposed to a passion. As for me, my answer was straightforward. Legacy made me happy, allowing me to live life on my terms. I hoped my parents would see the differences in the answers inspired by the mindset of each of their children. I don't know if they did or not. But based on the data Terry and his team presented to my parents, they were able to advise us as to the best plan of action. Even with the plan in hand, it still took three years from the time of the assessment to get my dad fully on board.

A change in the federal estate tax laws played a key role in his resistance. Originally, estate taxes were levied on amounts over $5.6 million.[24] At the time, it was increased to $11.58 million, and as of 2024, the amount is $13.61 million.[25] My dad saw this and said

---

24   "A Brief History of Estate Taxes," Pennsylvania Advisory Services, accessed May 28, 2024, https://www.paadvisory.com/resource-center/estate/a-brief-history-of-estate-taxes.

25   Ben Geier, CEPF. "Pennsylvania Estate Tax," SmartAsset.com, accessed May 28, 2024, https://smartasset.com/estate-planning/pennsylvania-estate-tax.

there was no need to transition the company because he didn't have $11 million. I mentioned that the company could easily grow to that amount. He cut off the conversation and then said he didn't think we needed to transition the company any longer. In response, I walked out of that family meeting, went to my office, grabbed my jacket, purse, and keys, and closed my office door.

On my way out, I passed the conference room, didn't look in, walked out the front door, got in the car, and went home. I downed a bottle of prosecco, drinking straight out of the bottle, and watched Bravo for the rest of the day. Had I had a match—and the building was empty, of course—I would have thrown it over my shoulder like Angela Bassett's character did in the movie *Waiting to Exhale*. That's how mad I was! As I was nursing that bottle of prosecco, I couldn't help but ask myself over and over, "What am I going to do?" I'm not an ultimatum person unless I am willing to live with the alternative. I thought about all the time and energy I'd invested, everything I'd put on pause, and all the sacrifices. Truthfully, those thoughts made me salty with my parents.

The next day, though, I pushed my anger aside to help a family member in need. When you have a successful family, you are often called upon to help others. I showed up as the consummate professional I am to handle business. Because that's who I am—the reliable child. Did I want to? No. Did I speak to my dad? No. Did I do what I was supposed to do? Yes. There was never an apology or even a mention of the conversation. I, of course, went back to the office the following Monday. A few weeks went by. Then, as if Black Jesus came from the sky and whispered in his ear, my dad said to me, "You know, Karla, I was thinking. If I were you, I wouldn't want to give up all my time, energy, and assets only then to immediately write off 66 percent of the proceeds. You're right." That's how the whole thing ended, and we are where we are today. It took me, holding on to what I knew to be right, and Black Jesus.

As for the hesitancy of my parents, I think they had to realize with the help of Terry that *fair* and *equal* are two different things. I get it. They wanted to be fair to all three of their children. I believe they felt that allowing me to take over the business and not my brothers would be saying to them that they love me more. With the help of Terry and his team, I believe my parents saw that their focus needed to be shifted from their children to what was best for the organization—not necessarily what was fair.

I didn't judge my parents for believing the way they did. I got it and was able to see the duality of it. They didn't want to make it seem as if they were biased toward me by "giving" me the company. But I believe they were conflating a business decision with a measurement of love or, worse yet, nepotism. If I were "given" the company, it would mean to my brothers that their love tilted more in my favor. But this is where Terry and his team were so beneficial. They shared an alternative view and multiple options with my parents. They showed them that fair does not mean equal. They showed my parents how leaving other assets in the estate plan could even it out. To that point, my taking over the company could be seen as me purchasing my inheritance even though my parents were both still living. I just got my share on the front end.

And it wasn't "given" to me. I have a *huge* loan I am still paying off to this day. I have to work not just to maintain the business but to grow it. I'm not stripping down the company for cash; I'm using it as a tool of economic stability and generational wealth for our family. I am continuing the Electro Soft–Wallace family legacy.

When COVID-19 Enters the Chat

I remember going through this process like it was yesterday. When I finally signed the papers in January 2020, I turned to Terry and said in jest that we'd finally made it through to the finish line. He looked at me stoically and said words that still haunt me to this day. I'm joking … but not really.

He looked at me and said, "Be careful of what you wish for."

His words hung in the air, and I shook his hand and tried to shake off his words. He'd given my father and me a bottle of champagne each. That was on a Friday, and we both were back to work on Monday. There was no party or big celebration dinner. I think I took that bottle of champagne to a diner with my husband on Sunday of that weekend to at least commemorate the occasion. I should have done more, but it was really anticlimactic.

Everything continued to run smoothly until March, when the world came to a standstill. COVID-19 entered the equation. I had always thought that my preparation and training prepared me for a time like this—or at least to be as ready as I could be. This was different from anything any of us had ever seen. We were able to keep our full staff on during that transference, and my main concern was taking care of them. As I think back on how I had to juggle everything through that situation—dealing with the bank, making sure my people were OK—as I navigated all the PPP (Paycheck Protection Program) regulations, I couldn't help thinking of my brothers.

I couldn't see them calling the bank guy on a Sunday, trying to figure out the portal, drilling down information for our payroll processor, and doing financials. To be fair, none of us knew what to do. My accountant, my father, my banker—we were all trying to figure it out. Plus, my two middle school sons had to now have two quiet areas set up in the new house we had just purchased because school was now online. Everything was new, different, and chaotic. But this was the job and life that I signed up for. I am unstoppable when it comes to making things happen. I just figure things out. That is the job of a second-generation CEO.

Reflection Points

• **See your family's business transition for what it is and not what you want it to be.**

When dealing with family during a business transition, it's easy to get emotional. This may stall the business transition activities. Try your best not to let those emotions stay and slow—or worse, halt—progress. The company is the priority. The predominant question that should be foremost in each family member's mind is "What's in the best interest of the organization?" Answering this crucial question will save time and alleviate any hurt feelings. The proof will be in the data.

• **Never be afraid to walk away if everything that you need to make you happy and complete is not in the package.**

Don't feel pressured to be in a situation that doesn't serve you for the benefit of others. Look, don't just leave at the first sign of resistance either. What I'm saying is that this will be a process, but don't lose your desired outcome in the midst of it.

• **Call in reinforcements**

There is no way my family and I would be where we are with Electro Soft without the help of Terry and his team. I write this in the fullest confidence. They were just what we needed, a third party whose intention was to aid us and guide us to the best decision possible. Our success was predicated on their knowledge, and it was as cohesive as I could have hoped for. Find the best team for you and your family.

• **Honestly assess where your family is.**

My father talked about retiring for eleven years. Although he didn't come right out and say it, his actions were clear. There was some hesitancy there, and he needed some help getting comfortable. I realized this because I watched him and listened with a CEO's ear to the words he was saying. I looked at him with the eyes of a fellow executive, not as his daughter. Can you honestly view your family members as business associates who happen to be family instead of family members whom you do business with? If the answer to the second question is no, go back and read the point before this one. You've got to get to a place where your main concern is the legacy of the business and not falling out of favor with your family. That is the generational CEO's mindset.

CHAPTER THREE

What Does It Mean to Be a Woman in Manufacturing?

You can't wait for someone to dub you CEO. You have to start acting like the CEO, making the decisions that the CEO needs to make. You shouldn't be waiting for some future time to pull out your good stuff. You should always be demonstrating the A game, making the rules, and saying what you're going to say the way a leader would say it.

—Karla Trotman, CEO of Electro Soft

My first experience seeing a woman running her own business was my maternal grandmother, Shirley Burton Scott. She ran Burton's, a store that was also a restaurant in a Black neighborhood called North Hills, which was basically Glenside, Pennsylvania. It was a magical place for me. I remember being little and my cousin Joyce would make a little bed on the second-level floor for me out of the plastic crates that hamburger buns and hoagie rolls would come in. She would make it comfortable by putting in blankets. I was small at the time and could fit perfectly inside one.

I can still see the store in my mind. I remember the orange countertops, the sounds of the cash register ringing, me and my cousins playing store. Then there was the smell. The aroma of burgers and french fries wafted from the first floor, where my grandmother cooked for us and the patrons of her restaurant. Burton's was the place to be! Everyone in town knew my grandmother and loved her. The energy in there was electrifying!

Ironically, she hadn't even wanted to start a store, but her husband, my grandfather, convinced her to open it. And when he got sick, my mom would drive down from college on the weekends to work in the store. It was the ultimate family business. And there I was, a little girl, soaking it all in like a sponge.

I got my MBA from Drexel University, but from my grandmother I got a "kitchen table MBA." She taught me how to take care of customers by making them feel seen and giving them quality service. She also taught me to know who I was and stand my ground. You may have noticed that quality in me from the last chapter. As a woman in business, I believe that our biggest strength is seeing the humanity in business and using it as a strength, not a weakness. Also, I learned from my grandmother to be proud of what I produce by always bringing my A game and to stand on integrity.

Most importantly, through her I saw the unifying power of business, not just with clients but also within work teams as well. A reciprocal exchange occurs in business along with a mutual exchange of respect. Her tried-and-true lessons and what I learned from my parents are what prepared me for ownership in such a highly male-dominated industry.

That's what I want to impart in this chapter to every woman. There is no need to be something that you are not or attempt to fit into any mold. I don't think I've ever truly fit into any space. I've always felt out of place until I realized that it was just my energy disrupting the status quo. Never question your right to be in any space because of someone else's limiting beliefs, ideas, or thoughts of you.

I can't help but think of the pioneering hair product manufacturer Madame C. J. Walker, who became our nation's first self-made female millionaire in the 1800s. As she rose to prominence, she literally was in a lane of her own. While throughout history many women worked in manufacturing, revitalizing the workforce while men fought in wars, very few women have been in an ownership capacity the way Madame C. J. Walker was.

Unfortunately, her business fell into the category of many Black-owned family businesses that don't continue into a second generation, but she still holds the distinction of being the biggest female name in United States manufacturing industry history. Although she blazed the trail, few have followed in her footsteps. But she is among the great women manufacturers who have impacted my path.

My place in manufacturing may surprise many, but it was not hard for me to acclimate to an industry lacking female representation. Finding my place in manufacturing was actually somewhat seamless. Having transitioned from business logistics, I was used to frequently being "the only one" in most business scenarios. As a Black woman, you tend to get used to the reactions of others in an initial interaction.

First, if you are a successful Black woman, you're most likely familiar with the surprised looks they try to cover, not realizing that their surprise is written on their faces. But when I found my way to manufacturing, the subtle glances I used to get became full-blown looks and, in some cases, stares. As I think of it, the only time I realize

I'm an anomaly is when I see the manifestation of it worn on the faces when I walk into the room.

Before manufacturing, I'd jokingly compare the effect of my walking into rooms as Bigfoot making a rare appearance. Manufacturing, however, calls for a more extreme example. It's now more like a "Bigfoot riding a purple unicorn over the head of the Loch Ness Monster" type of uniqueness. I get it. The reality is that there just aren't a lot of women in manufacturing. Here's why the stares are so prevalent. In a snapshot gender comparison, manufacturing is 67.9 percent male and 30.0 percent female.[26] Then women are rarer in management roles and at C-suite executive levels in the industry. According to recent manufacturing industry data polled by the US Census, one in four women hold management positions, and 12 percent hold C-suite positions.[27]

If you want to niche down even further to ownership, the data—the percentage of manufacturing firms owned by women, not to mention Black women—simply doesn't exist. So, it's understandable why meeting a Black woman who owns a manufacturing firm and also serves as the president and CEO will turn some heads and conjure some interest.

Holding a unique place in the industry does create an interesting set of challenges. At conventions and in networking spaces after hours, other attendees may assume that you are there just to be "arm candy." This assumption is in stark contrast to the perception of my male predecessor at Electro Soft—my dad. Then there's finding mentorship, facing challenges in business banking and financing spaces, and being the hidden option in the black hole of diversity, equity, and

---

26   Earlene K. P. Dowell, "Manufacturing Opens More Doors to Women," United States Census Bureau, accessed November 19, 2023, https://www.census.gov/library/stories/2022/10/more-women-in-manufacturing-jobs.html.

27   Dowell, "Manufacturing Opens More Doors to Women."

inclusion. Being a Black woman CEO in manufacturing is a veritable obstacle course. This chapter will explore workarounds I've created and hopefully will add a little light to the presently bleak reality of women in manufacturing.

Acquiring Growth and Using Tactics

Client matriculation and retention are the fundamentals of building and maintaining a secure business. Without acquiring new business, your company will not make it. I know this statement may seem obvious, but I find that other female CEOs, especially those starting out, need to be reminded of the effort and ingenuity it takes to represent and sell your company. A true CEO does not just rely on the abilities of their trained sales staff. You have a role to play as well, and a major one, in ensuring that the company services the best clients. Admittedly, as a woman, there are some biases you must sidestep to get to where you want to be in terms of your bottom line.

Again, I want to give anyone who reads this chapter the resources they need to feel comfortable selling in any arena and to close the deals they need with confidence and a bit of strategy. Whether the sales take place in person, over the phone, or in videoconferencing, there are multiple ways to make it happen for your benefit.

A major component for anyone in business, not just women, is industry conferences. To become a thought leader or prominent name within your specific industry, it's best to interact on a higher level with your colleagues nationally. However, as a woman in business attending a conference, the situation can be a little bit unique. I use the word *unique* because I feel like that's the best way to positively describe it.

Let me provide an example of what I mean. At any given convention, as I browse the different tables or go to the different breakout sessions and we get to the networking portion, typically I'm approached by men, and the intention isn't always professional. The initial conversation always starts the same way. A fellow convention attendee will ask me, "So, who do you work for?"

Instead of saying that I work for my company Electro Soft, I tell them that I work for myself. Once I say that, the conversation shifts totally. That one detail, my sharing the ownership component, allows me to be seen in a brand-new light. Shifting the intended approach of someone is something I'm sure my male industry counterparts do not deal with as much as women in manufacturing. It's not disrespectful as much as it is standard and typical when it comes to female representation at these conferences.

When the after-hour networking cocktail hour begins, another dynamic presents itself as a different situation. I've been in a group of colleagues chatting when a new joiner of the group, assuming I am someone's wife, will ask me who I'm with. I call it the "arm candy effect." The first thought that comes to their mind is that I'm here with the executive and not *the executive*. Unfortunately, the truth is that I've learned to lower my standards when it comes to the outcome of these conferences.

That statement is not to undermine the integrity of the conference planning or its operational staff by any means. It is a commentary on the representatives of the attending companies who are present at these conferences. They could be more inclusive to attendees who are unlike themselves. It's unfortunate, because when utilized properly, conferences can be a way for employers to cultivate new emerging and diverse talent. But if a woman is not taken as seriously as her male counterparts, then the opportunity is lost.

So, because these conferences are so unpredictable, I create a strategic game plan to get the conversation to go where I want it to go. It's a conversation devised using old-school sales methods. Before starting any conference exchange, I employ a technique that I call "show the double incentive." Essentially, it's starting with one major benefit and tying it to an associated benefit that will yield a profitable outcome. The following example works for companies when they make a statement about wanting to diversify a part of their business. Because I am a Black business owner, I could just make it all surface and about them hiring a company with a diverse workforce. This is important, but there are deeper levels I can take it to.

I lead first with their diversifying an aspect of their business. Let's take the supply chain, for instance. Among the lessons we learned as business owners from the shutdown in 2020, one of the biggest was its effect on getting materials to suppliers and then to consumers. It's always good to have an additional option for supply. I use this technique on companies that really want to diversify their supply chain. When they do want to pull me into a business-based conversation, I lean into my strategy knowledge. Like when I tell them our top-line revenue, and they respond that their existing vendor's current orders usually are the same as my top-line revenue.

Their implication is that we are in essence too small to take on all the work. But in reality, what we're asking for is to simply take a segment of the project. What that does is initiate a diversification strategy for them. That helps us slowly initiate a relationship of trust while "dating one another," simultaneously building a stronger relationship over time.

At this point in the industry, it doesn't make sense for any company not to diversify its supply chain. I convey that with a single source of supply, anything could happen. I must really convince them that this is an opportunity, not just to give a diverse company a chance but really to think about their supply chain in a different way. This explanation requires me to go into sales persuasion mode, asking them for the opportunity to show them our high quality of work. The great fallacy is that a lot of prospective clients sleep on our ability to actually do the work. There is an unconscious bias surrounding highly technical products and who can build them. It's societal programming. The reality is that diverse companies can and are doing these projects globally. This diversification strategy is a great way to start the conversation and tilt it in Electro Soft's favor.

It's been the case that most of the tried-and-true companies that have been clients for years are the companies that we've acquired in that way. It's been a major part of our success. Developing your specific best practices will ensure growth. Simultaneously, it's important to have a vision for where you want your company to go. Stagnation and lack of vision equate to the death of your company.

For Electro Soft, future growth looks like securing government contracts (which could be a whole chapter), increasing the workflow that we're doing currently with our suppliers, and then going through this long, circuitous song and dance of entertaining new business. But thankfully I have the success of my dad to build from. His growth story is distinct from mine. Ironically, when my dad started, he joined together with a white business partner who served as his vice president. Their partnership was symbiotic because my dad was the engineer and the VP was more the sales guy. But when potential customers visited the office, the VP was the first face they saw as the "front man." The assumption was that he was in charge. But the person they needed to speak to would be my dad, because he was the engineer.

Traditionally, people think my dad is Cuban or Latino because of his complexion and hair texture. For the most part, they never assumed he was an engineer. The white business partner was the face of the business. This setup was an unconscious bias workaround, providing the assurance companies needed to give Electro Soft a chance. The work spoke for itself. The company operated in this capacity for years. Even after his partner's untimely passing, it wasn't until 2008 that we felt confident enough to put my dad's picture on the website. It was never front and center before then.

The challenge today still is getting people and consumers to see that Black-owned and women-owned businesses can do highly technical, sophisticated manufacturing. It affects how people see, hear, and think about things. It's tough to combat entrenched stereotypes, but when you let the excellence of your work establish your business reputation, the client base grows organically.

If I am honest, I vacillate between whether to use my image on the website. As of the writing of this book, it is there, and because of the power of word of mouth, we are grateful to be successful. At times I can't help but wonder, were I in the start-up phase, if I would have the same success using my image. If you're reading these pages and are not sure what tactic will work best for your business's success, consider your industry and its clientele. As it relates to the online presence of your company and your desire to be in manufacturing as a woman, you have options. You can make a strategic decision like my dad and play from a power position in the background, ensuring you put yourself on the growth path. And when you hit your rhythm, you can become the face of the company as your business continues to scale. As always, the choice is yours, but you have control over the way your company will be perceived.

Establishing Yourself as an Authority

This next section, although truthful, has some delicate elements in it, but I'm going to go there because it's the reality that women business owners in barrier industries face. It's been so inflammatory recently in the private business sector with the all-out war regarding the entitlement of grant funding, financing, and equal opportunities. Yet the same debate and verbal sparring do not occur when discussing the inequality of experience and education standards that make someone a success in their industry.

Specifically, authority and credibility as validated by formal education are mandatory to a greater degree for some demographics than others. For women to be taken seriously and be competitive in their respective marketplace, they must have exceptional educational accolades. Other demographics are given the benefit of the doubt simply by existing and exerting basic effort. It doesn't take much for them to be viewed as key players in their industry.

For women, the cards are stacked a bit differently. We are tasked with building authority. Then, even though we know we have knowledge, at our most competent levels there's always going to be an attempt from someone trying to downplay us and make us feel that we are the imposter. I've experienced this and personally know many women who have gone through this as well. This negates all the hard work we've done to get to where we are.

Even though we are in the work, being identified, noticed, awarded, and called upon for our expertise, there are always going to be people who doubt us, and if not, you begin to doubt yourself. For me, I find that I ask myself, "What am I missing?" And when I'm working through the really big problems at the company, I take a beat and think to myself, "Why can't I figure this out?" I always think there's more that I can do. I feel like there was something I was supposed to have read and paid attention to in an article, book, podcast, or something that I could have delved into to get me to the answers that I needed. I want to know ... Where are the experts I can call? Who can help me through this issue? How much money can I throw at it?

I'm obsessed with the success of Electro Soft. Sometimes when things get particularly challenging, like during the COVID-19 shutdown, I truthfully was nervous and very scared. Self-doubt was at an all-time high. All I could do was take in all the information I could, listen to those who could help, and keep my people in the loop. Essentially, I had to stand strong amid the chaos. One of my favorite Brené Brown quotes is "In the absence of data, we will always make up stories."[28]

So, I increased communication. I didn't want our workforce to feel lost and disconnected or become fearful for their livelihood. I felt in that moment that we all grew together. The staff members were able to see how I work under fire, and I built their trust along the way. I pushed through my doubts and was proactive instead of being reactive. But regular people outside your organization don't know you in that capacity and make plenty of assumptions about you. There will be doubt about who you are. As long as those working alongside you—and, most importantly, you—know the truth, that's all that matters. Eventually you find your groove, and the doubt falls away. But yes, it is one of those unfair and unfortunate elements that women deal with as they build authority across many industries—not only manufacturing.

BE INFORMED

It wasn't until I had gone back to graduate school that I really developed the desire to read and be more informed about management, leadership, and finance. Reading books and having an executive

28 Goodreads, Brené Brown Quotes, accessed May 28, 2204. https://www.goodreads.com/quotes/8657163-in-the-absence-of-data-we-will-always-make-up.

coach who would assign readings helped inform me. This knowledge enabled me to be aligned with current industry standards. Additionally, books have literally changed my life and the way I think about Electro Soft, wealth, and business interaction. I encourage you to read and consume podcasts on an ongoing basis. Your knowledge can be your biggest asset.

Frequently, I get asked what my must-read business books are. I've compiled them for you in a partial list as a companion to this book. You can check it out on my website, which you can visit by scanning the QR code below.

Scan to get my list of must-read business books.

OBTAIN MENTORSHIP

To get information independently, it's important to obtain mentorship. Getting a mentor may be easier said than done working in manufacturing. There are not many women who we can ask to guide us due to the lack of representation. I've had some great mentors, and I have one currently, but finding them didn't happen on a whim. It took a concerted effort to ask within my networks. My business associations have proven to be an asset to me on so many levels. I talk more about finding the right groups for you along your CEO journey in the next chapter, but I urge you to ask for what you need from those you interact with frequently.

Establishing relationships in an industry where you are solo is a vital part of your growth. It helps to have alliances and guidance. As the only Black woman in manufacturing, and in my CEO group in general, I relied heavily on their expertise. They had access to information that I did not have during the COVID-19 shutdown, which enabled me to take care of my team and my business. So, if you are having difficulties finding a mentor, use the resources you have available to you in the meantime. By attending conferences, forums, workshops, and state-funded events, you'll eventually align with industry-specific help.

TAKE A STAND

Third, don't be afraid to do things differently from other CEOs who've come before you, but at the same time, take care of your people. As I was transitioning from being known as the daughter of the CEO to being CEO, I had to shift a lot of expectations in our people. At Electro Soft, we pride ourselves on having a high level of retention in our workforce. Some of our people have been working with us for years. I treat everyone here as my family and take care of them. They are a part of the legacy I am upholding for this business.

During those last three years of my father's retirement, as he was stepping down, what they didn't know was that I was running the business predominantly during that time. When he officially announced his retirement, he told them that if they liked how the business was run for the past three years, then they'd be satisfied with the transition, because I was the one behind all the operations. Being here in the new capacity, I knew I had to win their trust. Some people were fine with the changes, and others weren't. Either way, I was supportive of their choice to leave or to stay on. (No one left.) I had my vision of where I wanted the company to go and worked toward their buy-in.

Along that line, when you reach a modicum of success, your interpersonal and family relationships will shift a bit as well. Some people in your life will operate on the misguided assumption that your assignment on Earth is to be their personal finance department. They feel you have what they perceive as a substantial amount of money, and they don't have as much. In their mind it is your obligation to help them, because what they lack is context. In reality, with mo' money comes mo' bills.

Look, being able to help family and friends in need is a blessing, but I caution you to not become other people's financial savior. That is a tough game to play and to sustain. View this as an opportunity to coach them on how to make better money decisions. Don't get in the habit of throwing good money after bad habits. Often where the education system has failed us is in teaching cash flow and money management knowledge. Your help should come in the form of not just a check but also a plan to make better decisions.

Another reality is that your friend circle may shift a bit. When taking on the responsibility of running a business, suddenly your concerns have different levels to them. The things that keep me up at night are not the things that most people think about or worry about. I find myself thinking about interest rates and how they will affect the economy or my line of credit. Then there are the thoughts that awaken me from sleep in the middle of the night, like how to round out employee benefit packages so that we remain competitive, attract amazing prospects, and keep them.

Those conversations are not interesting to friends who work in corporate America. I have memories of conversations that suddenly shifted to a new topic shortly after I began sharing what was going on with my business. I assume it's because what I have to say is not interesting or is hard to relate to. I get it!

Over the years I've learned that I simply needed a set of business-owning friends who were aligned with my goals. My business-owning friends have the same challenges and concerns. We are all passionate about many of the day-to-day issues that impact business. These same friends bring a wealth of experience and a vast network of resources and connections. It's funny, but I didn't realize how hungry I was for like-minded individuals until I met them.

To bring this topic full circle, we talked about diversification earlier in the book. Do the same thing with your friend circles. Take the time to diversify your social and interpersonal relationships. It makes a huge difference in your life in more ways than you can imagine.

IMAGE MATTERS

Lastly, create your own image of how you show up as the CEO version of yourself, and don't feel pressured to change it to be accepted by someone else. What I mean is, as an executive, your appearance is scrutinized more than you may realize. Your team, workforce, clients, colleagues, and others are noticing you. You can't alter people's opinions of you, but you can control how you present yourself.

I remember my father always telling me that you must watch what you drive and what you wear because customers will think they're paying you too much. He urged me to be aware that those are the types of things they think about. But recently a mentor gave me conflicting advice, saying that at a certain dollar value, clients want to believe that you're a good steward of your money and that you are at least successful.

Somewhere between their thoughts, I learned to find my balance. Recently, one of my clients noticed my watch and asked me about it, noting the brand. For a second, I froze and wondered if I'd made a mistake. Usually I wear a wellness monitor as a watch, but I had an event that day and chose a dressier option. I was conflicted for a good five seconds, and then I made it up in my mind on the spot. Why should I hide the success of my company? Is this part of the game other people play, or do they not think anything of it because people expect them to uphold a certain standard?

My thoughts then shifted to some of the companies I work with. When I visit them, they've got their fancy cars parked outside, are wearing their high-end designer watches, and talk about the fabulous vacations they take. And yet I feel like I have to be—or I've been asked to be—demure, because it's almost as if people still can't accept the model of success that is in front of them.

Over the years, I've learned to disregard the assumption I've felt and heard repeatedly that for "us" to have nice things, we've gotten them through nefarious ways or by chance. It was my mentor who convinced me that at the level at which we were operating, clients want to know their money is being spent well, that the company is in good financial health, and that I'm a successful business owner. Why else would we make all of the sacrifices, leverage our assets, and spend countless nights worrying if we cannot enjoy the rewards? That was a brand-new mindset shift for me because I'd been hiding it for so long.

Oh, and the client who asked me about the watch then showed me his. It was from the same brand, and he was an associate of the company I was doing business with. As the owner, I paused as he asked me about my watch. But there he was, an associate, proudly wearing proof of his success.

Again, these are remnants of the effects of imposter syndrome with a side of respectability politics. It's hard to have a clear mind and not have these limiting beliefs when your head is filled with societal lessons and burdens. Heavy is the head that wears the crown at times.

The moral of the story is, people are conditioned to perceive different things, and their perception is none of your business. Make the choices that resonate the best with you and are authentic to who you are. Get comfortable with taking risks and being who you are in business.

Reflection Points

• Know that your presence in certain environments will surprise some people.

Take it in stride, and be present in every situation. You can maneuver conversations and exchanges and tilt them in your favor. Listen for the problem that a potential client may share with you, and come up with a strategy toward the solution. Your strength is your individuality and your ability to offer the client a new possibility. Your insight may make them see things in a way they never considered before. Use every interaction as an opportunity to develop this skill, and pretty soon it will become second nature. Create your plan, and work your plan as you work the room.

• Build your authority by putting in the work.

Learn. Grow. Don't judge yourself but discover how you can enrich your CEO experience by building and securing a knowledge base. Check out my list of must-read books, and read the ones that resonate with you. You can't help that people will doubt you. What you *can* do is make sure they know that you know your stuff. Learn and lead with your intellect.

• **Realize that limiting beliefs are real but that you don't need to dwell in them. Feel what you feel, and then release it quickly.**

There are but so many books you can read, courses you can take, and podcasts you can absorb to get the optimal answer or obtain perfection, which truly doesn't exist. There comes a point where you realize that you are enough. What you know is enough. You've put in the work to get to where you are. No matter how much progress you make, some people will never view you as an equal. Which is fine. It is your liberty to know who you are and to move into that space and let your work do all the talking for you.

• **Alleviate pressures from yourself by luxuriating in your authenticity.**

There is only one you, so show up as yourself. If you want to show your success in terms of luxury items or trips, then do it. You've paid the cost to be the boss. Live out loud, live freely, and live in the means that justify your happiness and your satisfaction. Understand that no matter what you do, there will be scrutiny, so you might as well do your thing. You are a part of an elite history of women who have come before you, and you set the precedent and tone for the women who will come after you. You are making history—so do it your way.

CHAPTER FOUR

How Do We Access Capital and Financing?

An Exploration into Acquiring Funding as a Black-Owned Business

---

Businesses don't fail; they run out of money.

—James Wallace, founder of Electro Soft

If you don't know by now, I "keep it 100," and this next chapter will keep that same energy. This chapter will not be an opinion-laden lecture. Instead, we'll go over the reality. Obtaining financing and capital as a Black business owner is complicated, but the one key component it requires is simple: facing the truth.

The truth is that the system is flawed, and the game of business is rigged. I'm going to share the historical and repetitive incongruencies with receipts. As we've done before, it's time again to use facts and numbers to shed light on an issue. In the United States, there are two million Black-owned businesses, yet only 1 percent of Black businesses obtain business loans in their first year. [29]

This financial abyss leads many Black business owners to use their personal funding to begin their businesses. It's ironic, because a business school curriculum teaches students not to start a business with their own money. The recommendation is to use other people's money. But I know that when I started my very first business, and when my dad and a lot of other people also started their businesses, they had no other choice or option. Not having access to other people's money left them to use their own money—and, as a last resort, credit cards, which is a big no-no—in business. That rule is practically Business 101 material.

However, despite the warning, feeling they have no choice, 44 percent of Black business owners use their own cash to start their venture.[30] But Black business owners know what's going on. Knowing their attempts to get funding will be heavily scrutinized, often with a fine-toothed comb, they stay away from lenders. Thirty-eight percent of Black business owners are discouraged from applying for loans.[31] The effort doesn't match the highly probable repeated outcome of denial.

This continual slap in the face causes a cyclically frustrating pattern. Entrepreneurship is potentially the gateway to financial access, stability, and generational wealth. But with a systemic obstruction to financial funding, it becomes the proverbial carrot dangling just out of reach of those wanting a better life. The cause is evident. A barrier exists between Black businesses and access to funding.

---

29   Nick Perry, "20 Black-Owned Business Statistics," Fundera by NerdWallet, January 23, 2023, accessed November 8, 2023, https://www.fundera.com/resources/black-owned-business-statistics#sources.

30   Perry, "20 Black-Owned Business Statistics."

31   Perry, "20 Black-Owned Business Statistics."

The truth is, the disparity that lies within the metrics of Black business funding versus majority- or white-owned businesses is astounding. To illustrate this with numbers, in 2019 only 31 percent of Black-owned businesses got their full requested amount to fund their business versus nearly 50 percent of white business owners, 39 percent of Asian owners, and 35 percent of Hispanic owners.[32] The reality is that 38 percent of Black-owned small businesses were denied the financing they applied for compared with 33 percent of Latino-owned businesses, 24 percent of Asian-owned businesses, and 20 percent of white-owned businesses.[33]

The inception of this inequality is woven into the fabric of our nation. From Black soldiers after World War II being denied access to the GI Bill by southern lawmakers to the crippling economic effects of the Jim Crow era until the mid-1960s, American Blacks have long felt the cold shut-out of economic discrimination.[34]

This is not just a Black American problem; it is a national issue causing division and inadequacies in the US economy. The estimated wealth gap between Blacks and whites in America potentially costs the economy between $1 trillion and $1.5 trillion in lost consumption and investment between 2019 and 2020, which translates to a GDP penalty of 4 to 6 percent.[35]

---

32 Taylor Avery and Samantha Masunga, "Black-Owned Business Face a System Set Up against Them. COVID-19 Makes It Worse." *Los Angeles Times*, June 20, 2020, accessed November 8, 2023, https://www.latimes.com/business/story/2020-06-20/black-owned-business-loans-banks.

33 Avery and Masunga, "Black-Owned Business Face a System Set Up against Them. COVID-19 Makes It Worse."

34 Joseph Losavio, "What Racism Costs Us All," *Finance & Development*, accessed November 8, 2023, https://www.imf.org/en/Publications/fandd/issues/2020/09/the-economic-cost-of-racism-losavio.

35 Losavio, "What Racism Costs Us All."

Although many Americans, politicians or otherwise, turn a blind eye to the inequalities, there are some organizations that see them and want to do their part to help. Organizations like Hello Alice and the Fearless Fund make it their mission to assist Black entrepreneurs to level the slanted playing field.

But as the adage goes, no good deed goes unpunished, as both organizations faced discrimination lawsuits in 2023 for their efforts to help Black—and the double-minority demographic, Black female—entrepreneurs.[36] In defense of their lawsuit against Hello Alice, the privately-owned activist entity American First Legal states that "Diversity, Equity, and Inclusion" are "gentle-sounding euphemisms [that] are designed to mask a brute force agenda of social engineering, Marxist dehumanization, and overt racism and sexism."[37]

So, let's do a quick recap. Black entrepreneurs are disproportionately denied funding from banks and other funders. So, an organization striving to do its part to combat this injustice is accused of social engineering by two members of the racial group that have a 50 percent chance of being awarded the funding they apply for. Make it make sense. The math is not math-ing. These organizations are being attacked because it's almost as if the "powers that be" don't want us to be on a level playing field—or allowed on the field, period. It's as if the rules we've been allotted are designed to have us fail at every turn, yet we've learned how to manipulate them to win simply the crumbs being left on the proverbial table. Now even the crumbs are too much.

---

36   Geri Stengel, "Hello Alice Defends Grants for Black Entrepreneurs," *Forbes*, accessed November 8, 2023, https://www.forbes.com/sites/geristengel/2023/10/16/hello-alice-defends-grants-for-black-entrepreneurs/?sh=8d4f2de7e71d.

37   Carolyn Rodz, Elizabeth Gore, and Kelsey Ruger, "Hello Alice Is Being Sued for Our Commitment to You. Help Us Lift Up 5 Million Voices to Elevate the American Dream," Email, October 4, 2023.

That brings me to my next point. Although this topic is heavy, this chapter will not be all doom and gloom negativity either. I'll share solutions and actionable workarounds by using my company, Electro Soft, as a case study. We'll survey how we overcame various obstacles. I believe there is a potential light at the end of the tunnel. With determination, education, and ingenuity, Black businesses, with concerted effort, can make strategic moves to establish themselves. To be clear, these solutions do not negate highly stacked odds against Black businesses. These strategic ideas were created to show that working logically and with intention can often give way to a suitable outcome.

Become a Visionary to Find Funding

Imagine this. A last-minute errand popped up for me on a busy afternoon, causing me to run to my bank to make a quick transaction for my business. This visit wasn't planned; it just ended up being one of the many additions to my already packed day. With me sporting a graphic tee and jeans and my hair in cornrows, I stated my intention to make a withdrawal to the bank teller. To be clear, it was a substantial sum of money, but for a business owner, it's what is necessary from time to time. Also, I'd been a member of this bank for a good amount of time, so I thought nothing of the request. That was, until the teller inquired why I was withdrawing that amount of money. *My money.*

And that was not the only time that happened at that branch and others. Then there were instances when I needed something notarized. Sometimes I was able to do it from the drive-up window, and other times I was asked to come into the branch. It's not like my coming into the building lends me any more credibility than being at the window with my identification. But the takeaway here is what I did.

Instead of suffering with that mistreatment in silence, I dialed the bank's market president, with whom I had a relationship, and reported my experience. He assured me that it would never happen again. That relationship with the market president was formed in part due to how hands-on I was in selecting a bank when I became CEO of Electro Soft. I knew it was important for me to have my own banking relationship outside the one my father had built with the bank he was using when he was CEO.

I found my chosen bank by coming at the situation intentionally and with a vision. I knew that a bank cannot control its frontline workers, nor could an afternoon of diversity, equity, and inclusion (DEI) training change a lifetime of preconceived notions. What I wanted was the power to go to the top to report exactly what was happening. I wanted access and to make sure my voice was being heard. It is important that those of us who have access use it to make it easier for those who do not. I feel it's a duty for me to advocate in those spaces in order to make it easier for those coming after me. Again, I was intentional.

Later on, I'll go into deeper detail about how important it is as a business owner to be seen and to interact within the community. For now, I'll mention how one such interaction in the community got me to the aforementioned bank. I sit on the board of a museum, and at the time I was on its corporate advisory council.

One evening they had a gathering on the museum terrace after a meeting. I was in the process of taking over the business, and I knew that I needed a solid banking relationship—preferably one with access to the top if I had issues on a branch level. My true desire was to have a partner who understood my goals and aspirations around Electro Soft. Mind you, we had a solid relationship at the time with a regional favorite.

Unfortunately, it did not align with the vision I had for the transaction, so I started meeting other banks' leaders, explaining to them the succession plan and requesting what I was looking for: a commercial loan. The day of the corporate advisory council, I had already received the term sheets from a total of six banks. At the event, I met a gentleman who just happened to be the market president from bank number seven. I told him who I was and what I was looking for, and he replied simply, "We'd love to give it a shot." Just like that.

He was just a nice guy, and on a nice afternoon, he confirmed he wanted my business off that single conversation. I told him that I was looking to move quickly. He responded that he could get me a term sheet within the week. This was a completely different reaction from banks one through six. Each of the other institutions eagerly wanted my business, but each of them wanted me to go through the Small Business Administration (SBA) lending route.

I feel it necessary to mention that when I bought the company, it was a thirty-one-year-old business with at least $1 million worth of equipment. I had assets and multiple retirement accounts to collateralize the ask, yet they pushed me off to SBA financing. I'm grateful that SBA financing exists because it has helped many, but I didn't think we needed it because my father, who was financially stable, was going to be my guarantor. Yes, my father backed the money that I was giving to him as my payment for the business.

Bank number seven, the bank I chose, didn't mention SBA. Now, they didn't give me everything I asked for, but they came very close. Even though I was able to provide proof of financial security with assets and had my father act as my cosigner, I still only got 75 percent of my ask, which at the present day I'm due to pay off over a year ahead of schedule. This is evidence that the barrier exists for all Black business owners regardless of what assets we do and don't have.

Getting back to finalizing my banking relationship, when I shared information about this bank to my team at the advisory firm, they gave me a head nod and stamp of approval. They loved my contact from the bank and the way the bank operated overall. They had faith that the relationship would be a good one and that we'd figure out how to make up the rest of the purchase price.

Now, let me share a dose of reality that can occur as you search for the bank you want. As with any aspect of business, it's best to exercise a certain amount of caution. A trusted colleague, someone whom I considered a business friend, also gave me a term sheet. The advisory team thoroughly reviewed it. When they finished, they advised me not to go with his bank. The team did their due diligence and discovered that the referred bank, where ironically my contact also worked, was having a lot—actually, a tremendous number—of issues at the time. My team couldn't in good faith allow me to do business with them.

I was brokenhearted that someone in my network—who'd met my father, had intimate knowledge of our business, and had even visited our company—was trying to put me with a banking institution that was in trouble. To be clear, he knew the compromised status of where they were as a business, and he put his interests before our professional relationship. To make matters worse, after I went in another direction, I found out he stopped working at the bank. He was going to leave me on a sinking ship! The entire situation was unfortunate.

Thankfully, I had a team in place to go over everything for me so that I didn't make a big mistake. Having a strong team of trusted advisors is a major benefit. The proof is evident in my situation. My current bank has really helped me think about finances differently and utilize its banking tools effectively. Remember the issues with the tellers? My effort in establishing a connection is how I was able to go to the top, the market president, with my complaint. I made the connection with him at a random event on a nice night on a terrace. Connection matters.

Since I've gone into my banking story, it's only fitting to talk about my dad's financing story as the first CEO of Electro Soft. It was the 1980s, and he was overseeing the design, manufacturing, and writing of software for blood analysis equipment. His particular division was losing money because they couldn't stabilize the manufacturing costs, so he suggested outsourcing the manufacturing piece to a "job shop."[38] That way they could have consistent costs. His idea was quickly dismissed.

Naturally, the company wound up being acquired, and the acquiring company shut them down because they weren't making money. My dad had a choice to stay and try to find a job under the premise that it's easier to find a job if you have a job, or he could take his severance and leave. And he took the severance and left.

While deciding his next steps, he was enjoying his free time. He was fishing and riding his bike, all the while knowing he'd just get another corporate role somewhere else. He'd become known in the area for his manufacturing knowledge, so one day someone called him and asked him to build a couple of cables. The company was very pleased with his work and asked him to build more cables.

That little job was the start of our family's company. Knowing that no banks were going to give capital to a Black man who walked into their doors starting a manufacturing company, he figured it'd be best to put some money behind it himself. He used his severance and the money from that very first project to seed the company. Because my mom and dad were the "friends and family" financing option that other family members came to for financial help, they didn't

---

38   Matics, "Glossary Terms: Job Shop Manufacturing," accessed May 8, 2024, https://matics.live/glossary/job-shop-manufacturing/.

have anyone in their circle to go to. They became their own in-house financing. Together, they had a vision.

Creating Your Funding Pathway

Even though time has passed, not much has changed when it comes to the scrutiny banks and lenders use toward Black-owned businesses. As you consider seeking funding, keep a couple of things in mind regarding banks. They look for a lot of different elements. You have to show who you are by building a relationship with them. They look at your taxes, what you own versus how much you owe and your ability to pay your bills, and your résumé and experience; they need to have faith that you can pay them back. If you are thinking that is a lot—the truth is, it is.

Once you've established your business, there are some alternate financial options to consider. Again, you know I'm going to be honest. The grant pool is drying up unless you have invented a unique product. If you are a service-based business as we are, it's helpful if that service is something other companies like to invest in. Private equity likes to put money into solid, steady businesses because of the steady profits.

Although manufacturing is not sexy like software, it is a steady industry, and private equity is drawn to us because our efficiency and the consistent demand for manufacturing continually trends upward. Although software may be more alluring, manufacturing is like that tried-and-true old-fashioned car that doesn't have a digital screen as a dashboard but will move you forward with stability. Investors like stability in a profile.

Other than outside investment capital, other buckets of money are available through various industry partnership grants. For instance, I joined a manufacturing industry partnership (IP) in my region. We are organized under our city's/county's workforce development office. In our particular partnership, the workforce development staff will write for industry-specific grants focused on workforce development, such as incumbent worker training or upskilling displaced workers.

The state government sets aside money to fund these grants. Our partnership must prove how the money will be spent, and then the funds are awarded to our partnership. Now, instead of my company utilizing all our budgeted training dollars, we are able to access funding through the IP. Here is an example of how it works. My staff requires training at a cost of $10,000. But I aso need $5,000 to invest in cybersecurity for my business. I submit a request to the IP for training funding. The IP accepts the request. I write a check to the training partner for the full $10,000. I submit proof of payment and training to the IP.

The IP refunds to my company a check for 50 percent of the cost of the training. The other $5,000 goes into a sustainability fund that can be used later by other companies. The sustainability fund allows the IP to continue to thrive in times when grant money is not as plentiful. Now I am able to fund the company's cybersecurity needs.

Another state-supported program that has been tremendously helpful is WEDnetPA, created by the Department of Community and Economic Development available through the Workforce and Economic Development Network of Pennsylvania.[39] It's a training program that allows businesses to allocate $2,000 per employee for training. Our industry trainings and certifications are extremely expensive, so this additional funding helps relieve the stress of deciding which employees should be trained or which project to fund. Again,

---

39 Pennsylvania Government, WEDnetPA Overview, accessed November 9, 2023, https://dced.pa.gov/programs/wednetpa/.

that extra bit of fund allocation allows you to invest the money you would have used for training toward another aspect of your business.

Now, I'm sure you see why being a visionary when finding financing is so crucial for the financial development of your business. To that point, being a Black business owner puts you in a landmark category for ingenuity, adaptability, and innovation. I hold this opinion because we are the strategic partners that other businesses should want to collab with—not just because of affirmative action or some performative pseudo-DEI initiative but because if they knew the things we went through just to be in business and stay in business, they'd realize we are the epitome of strategic partners.

We're the types of companies that make something out of nothing, with a perspective that could benefit any boardroom or corporate table. We're willing, and able, to face any challenge. We are Swiss Army knives. More on that later.

Be Seen: Step Outside of the Typical

There is a function of business ownership that I've seen other CEOs overlook—the importance of going out into the community and making a difference. Earlier I mentioned that I'm on the corporate advisory council of a museum. You might be thinking there is slim to no correlation between my participation on this board and manufacturing. That may be the case on a surface level, but my ideas, vision, and voice transcend the four walls of my business and my locale in the suburbs.

I knew that for me to make a name for the family business and myself, I had to get out from behind the desk and into the community. I had to give voice to what we were doing as a company and to my family's story. And what I found was that people were intrigued with our story. People love the fact that there was a Black-owned business where the daughter took over the company. Then on top of that, it's an electronics manufacturing business! It is such a unique situation. People want to know more.

Again, it's all about the story. When entering a new space, lead with your story. It should be something compelling and repeatable. A story that makes an impression on everyone you tell it to. Pretty soon my name was being mentioned in rooms and meetings that I didn't even attend. That is the power of getting outside your business and getting to know and meet the people. Look, don't be short-sighted, either. Think outside your daily parameters. It's not only getting outside your business in a physical sense but outside in terms of your industry. I could attend manufacturing conventions monthly or quarterly, but that would only get me so far. Honestly, some of the most fulfilling connections have happened in the least likely places and external industries from mine.

Also, think outside your local area. Seek these spaces in your region, state, and neighboring states, etc. Use social media to reach even more areas. It may seem like bragging, but I call it reminding people of what you do. If they hear it enough and see it, they're able to keep you top of mind for opportunities that may arise, such as board positions, speaking opportunities, and most importantly, business. Where you can have influence, those are the rooms you want to be in. Don't wait for an invitation. They aren't coming.

As a mentor once told me, nobody knows who you are and the amazing work you're doing. So, you have to go out and join things and be a part of what's going on. Show people who you are and the value you bring to the room and the conversation. In doing so, you have created social proof of your work. People sell the dream that awards and recognition from organizations don't matter, but they do.

They differentiate you from the competition and create opportunities for earned media placement. It allows you to be invited to do things that others aren't privy to and eventually solidifies you as an expert in your space.

When it comes to getting into those rooms, there is another skill I lean into. My authenticity. I don't get into these spaces just to parrot narratives and be the "vanilla" voice in the room; I bring my full self and opinions. People want *you* in the room, not your representative. It's about saying what needs to be said and calling things out when they are wrong. Those are the conversations you need to have. When your contributions are real and you lay out the truth, people respect your voice and see you're coming to the table with a unique perspective.

Even if there is no direct correlation, calls come in about opportunities from people I've never met. It's because of the instances when my work on boards, my story, and my reputation precede me. It's key that you know the environment you operate in and be willing to call a thing a thing, say what folks are thinking, or bring a unique/culturally relevant perspective to the table. Those are the voices that get heard. Listen, most of these proverbial tables are echo chambers, so the person thinking outside the box commands the space. No one needs to hear the same thing over and over again. Know this: people really want to work toward resolution or bring fresh energy into a group.

Any group that doesn't want to do so doesn't deserve your time or energy. I don't sit on those boards, and I don't recommend you do so either. If I see that the tone of the group is headed in the direction of complacency, I excuse myself from the organization and don't participate. I've learned that if it has no action, it has no power. Be selective with your time and energy. It matters. You want to feel as if you're able to give and receive in any effective group you join. The goal is always reciprocity.

One board I serve on, I am able to coach women on the continent of Africa. It is the most fulfilling experience of my morning. Those women have no idea how our time together enlightens me and energizes my spirit. That is why I do it. You will never get the opportunity to expand your reach until you explore new relationships across various groups.

An obvious place to look is business and networking groups where you'll find commonality and comradery. But again, I encourage you to step away from your normal behavior. We tend to select groups whose members look like us. But I want to challenge you to do it differently. Go for the groups that are aligned with your goals. That doesn't mean you should stay away from groups that match you from an ethnic standpoint. What I'm stating is, keep the same energy in finding aligned-business-goal groups. In the business-goal groups, we're not alike, but that's what makes it work. It makes the information fresh. Statistically, companies with diverse management and board members tend to excel at a higher rate than those that are homogenous. Diversity of thought creates conflict and draws out stronger solutions.

This modernized strategy is quite different from how businesses got funding back in the day. In the past, acquiring funding meant using educational connections and your relationships with your alma mater to get a nod or approval from other sources. Presently, many don't have those relationships and must look in spaces aligned with their funding and business goals. A good place to start is to ask within your existing network. I'm currently in a CEO group that was introduced to me through two successful manufacturers whom I admire. This group has been a tremendous source of information and guidance over the past five years. I pay a good amount of money to belong to this group.

This next point may step on someone's toes. But to get to the capital you need, it's necessary that I mention it. It takes money to make money. Sometimes you'll have to invest in these different groups with your time and money. Although I pay good money to be in some of the groups I'm in, it's worth it because I get tremendous value from each of them. Sometimes the value isn't obvious in the beginning, but in building relationships, I've learned how to leverage those connections. Good information is not always free, and free information is not always good. I'm all for a good hack now and then and doing things for free. But when it comes to learning best practices, it's best to pay for that information.

Be sure that there is a leader within whichever group or groups you choose. The group just can't be meandering around like sheep. Secondly, there needs to be a strong sense of accountability. You must be willing to call out your fellow members; in turn, you must also be comfortable with them calling you out when you are on some bs. I'll add this: pay attention to socioeconomics and experience. I've been in groups where the person who talked the most had the least experience and their business was barely performing. They were wasting everyone's time with untested advice.

Take the time to research and learn about the people with whom you are interacting. In my current CEO group, each person has been properly vetted. I researched each member and their businesses. Being in that place allows you to see the possibilities of strategic growth. It inspires me to take the company to the next level. My dad and I always say, "If you can see it, you can be it," so spend time with people who motivate you.

Next, I want to address any introverts who may be reading this and who want no part in putting themselves out there. The truth is that you must, for the sake of your company, be able to market yourself. Just find ways of marketing yourself that you don't mind doing. Maybe it's joining smaller groups or getting a business coach to help you. When looking for a coach, make sure you ask the necessary questions: "How many people have you helped successfully exit their company, and how many people have you made rich?" You want to make sure they are not just coaching as a hobby but rather that it's what they do. It's necessary that you come up with ways to get to your desired outcome.

If you picked up this book, I'm pretty sure you're aware of what it takes to pitch for capital, so you use that same drive to get out there and put your business into the spaces that matter. And if you're not the right person to pitch, I suggest you hire someone until you get better. Part of what wins money is people's belief in you. If they are intrigued by you, then they'll want to work with you. But whichever way works for you, make it your own. Maybe the introverted CEO is more comfortable with opening their business doors and letting people visit, sitting on smaller boards within the community, or maybe hosting events. You can develop a conference idea and let your marketing team take over. You can serve the purpose of getting the brand name out there and yet not be the face of it.

My father was that type of person. He did not like meetings or going places; in fact, he quit his CEO group because he said he had better things to do than sit around and listen to other people's problems. But in his defense, he was building a company from scratch. His work gave me an opportunity to get out there and work the rooms. We had gotten to a point as a company where we had done all we could do from a marketing perspective. It was time to get our name out there a bit more. This involved getting into the manufacturing network and starting to talk, not just listening to other people's problems. As the business went through different stages of growth, it continually called for different measures. So, it also depends on where a business owner or CEO, introverted or not, is with their business and what it needs.

Start with the End in Mind

Up to this point, there's been a lot of money talk. There is nothing wrong with that, because money plays a valuable role in your business health and personal and family well-being. But I urge you to find something deeper. Something that means more than just the pursuit of money. Making that "something" your final destination, your end, helps keep your mind on your journey. It helps determine how much money you will need and will be the fuel to remind you of what is ultimately your goal. My "something" is legacy. Legacy is a lot more important to me than money. Incrementally, I don't think one additional dollar per year would make me happier. There is no marginal utility in that. Legacy, however, is forever. My "something" may look different from yours. My "something" is about building up from what my parents started. Finding your "something," whether it's legacy or becoming the number one business in your sector, will keep you on track.

I am in the process of creating the life I would like to have and the legacy I would like to leave behind. For example, I like being able to do the things I like to do. I get excited about the future of Electro Soft and enjoy the process, challenges and all. I've defined what the happiness quotient is for me and how far I want to go in this journey, but I'm still not done figuring out my end game.

A colleague of mine in my CEO group offered me a new perspective when he informed me recently that the meeting we attended together would be his last. He had decided he was done growing his business. He'd built his company to the point where he had figured out how to put life on autopilot. He's happy and profitable. I admired that. He had determined where the end was for him.

Again, I feel like I'm just getting started, which is OK, but I appreciated seeing with my own eyes the true satisfaction that comes from meeting one's business goal. The moral of the story is you must determine what the end is for you. Don't get so caught up in reaching the next money goal that you lose sight of what matters.

Reflection Points

• **Finding capital and funding for a Black-owned family business has been a challenge, but it's not an impossibility.**

Become a visionary and do things differently to get different results. Own the task and get to it. Understand the obstacles before you, but don't let them inhibit you. You have more power than you realize. Your ingenuity and tenacity are your biggest gifts.

• **Step out of your bubble and find the money!**

Search for networking and executive groups of like-minded professionals where you will equally benefit from being in the room and contributing. Don't just gravitate to a group because of your comfort. Get in there and ask the tough questions, and make sure you'll benefit from being in the room. And don't just stay in your immediate area. Be creative and look in places you've never looked before. *Be seen!* Show up and show out! If you're serving on a board, let your voice be heard. Don't be a fly on the wall or be concerned with taking up space. What you contribute is unique and needed. If you're in the community, share your story. You never know who they know and how they can get you closer to achieving a goal.

• **Once your business is up and running, don't lose sight of what is important.**

Let's keep it real. Money is important, and it can add a lot of quality to your life and your business. However, it's not the be-all and end-all. Are you happy? What is your end goal? Considering these markers will let you know what your personal finish line is. I had to create my own "life KPIs," and it means that if those things are in alignment, all is well. Mine are helping my family, making sure the company is doing well, and seeing to it that our people are happy. My main KPIs are ensuring that I'm healthy in body and soul and friendships. I encourage you to be mindful of what you want in life, and setting life KPIs is a helpful hack.

CHAPTER FIVE

Which Strategies Ensure Effective Supply Chain Logistics?

Games are won or lost based on inches.

—Karla Trotman, CEO of Electro Soft

When we first began this journey in chapter 1, I mentioned that logistics was always a subject that was interesting to me. I liked it because it was a sector of business that wasn't boring. Not to shade accountants or insurance agents, but logistics is sexy. Consider the name. *Logistics.* It has a way of rolling off the tongue. And its predominant reputation in business as being a necessary component for success is impressive as well.

The Desert Storm war in the 1990s was won in part due to superior logistics. Then it appeared in my life in a personal capacity. My father, after serving active duty for four years in the US Air Force, returned to reserve duty, serving thirty years as a loadmaster. A loadmaster is the person responsible for getting cargo on the plane before a flight. What's cool was that the logistics component of his role required that he attend the Community College of the Air Force to obtain a logistics degree. So, as a little girl, I was always on the base seeing giant C-130 Hercules planes that he loaded and flew on. How could I not be fascinated?

Logistics makes a major impact on daily life too. Think about your favorite product at your local grocery store. There is a logistics system in place and a professional monitoring it to ensure the proper inventory of that item will satisfy the demand for it at the grocery store. As a reminder, logistics is defined as the movement of goods from one area to another strategically and symbiotically. Essentially, it's charting the path from extraction to consumerism of a product.

When I was considering higher education, I knew wherever I landed needed to have a solid logistics curriculum. That is what led me to Penn State University to study under one of the most renowned experts in business logistics, Dr. John Coyle. Although he's since passed, his ideology and grasp on the field remain with me and impact my career to this day. He was the reason Penn State grew to national recognition because of the pioneering logistical program he created.[40] That is why Penn State won my attendance above all the other institutions.

Despite Dr. Coyle's elevated stature of thought leadership, he was probably one of the most down-to-earth, real people I'd ever met in academia. This is quite a compliment, because stereotypically, professors are stuffy with an air of pretentiousness, but Dr. Coyle was a real dude. Even when it came to how he interacted with us. He was different.

For his lecture style, he used the Socratic method and posed questions to the class for topic exploration. When he started class,

40   Jim Carlson, "John Coyle, Pioneer of Penn State Business Logistics, Leaves Enduring Legacy," Smeal College of Business – Penn State, accessed March 27, 2024, https://www.psu.edu/news/smeal-college-business/story/john-coyle-pioneer-penn-state-business-logistics-leaves-enduring/.

you had to be on it. To keep up, you had to have deeply consumed all the materials and be ready when you stepped into his classroom. If not, you'd be embarrassed. His aim was for class to flow organically and conversationally. As I type this, I can see him now in my mind's eye at the front of the lecture hall, calling on different students and asking them their opinion on the assignment due for that day.

He kept us on our toes by engaging with us and causing us to use critical thinking skills. His education style thoroughly benefited me by teaching me how to think through issues—specifically supply chain issues. In the program at Penn State, we even learned the not-so-sexy part of logistics: stimulating subjects like transportation economics that taught concepts like congestion tolls.[41] Those subjects are necessary to fully understand logistics, but they are not sexy. But again, none of it was time or effort wasted.

Learning how to think through issues and concepts enabled me to troubleshoot all types of logistical concerns. Ironically, I didn't need the information I learned immediately after graduation, but it helped years later in times when the supply chains were affected. Thinking back on those days at Penn State, I was a bit ahead of my time. Back then, jobs were listed in the newspaper. There was no online search, and even if there was, I have a feeling it would have yielded the same outcome the newspaper did regarding the availability of logistic roles—nothing. Hardly any companies were looking to fill logistic roles. They didn't even exist. I returned to Penn State to use its resources. I obtained a list of companies that would possibly hire me. I printed a bunch of résumés and cover letters, sent them off in the mail, and followed up with phone calls.

---

41   "What Is Congestion Pricing?" Natural Resources Defense Council, accessed April 3, 3024, https://www.nrdc.org/stories/what-is-congestion-pricing.

Eventually, I found my first job after college by working in distribution in a warehouse on a second shift. It was a dark, dank warehouse with no windows, but landing this job helped me see things from another perspective. It allowed me to experience firsthand distribution within the logistics cycle. Building from the logistics definition mentioned earlier, let's examine the cycle further.

Let's use the retail clothing store The Gap as an example. The Gap has been in the clothing marketplace for fifty-plus years. Before a pair of their signature chinos or hoodies hits one of their hundreds of stores nationwide, the merchandise goes on a long journey before ending up on a hanger at your local store.

First, the clothing is made by a manufacturer overseas. Then the items are shipped overseas in a container. They then land at a port and are taken to a distribution warehouse. From there the clothes are separated by kind and then size. Then specific sizes are sent to certain locations and stores based on demand planning: the process of forecasting the quantity of product needed so that the right volume and sizes don't overburden the store. Those items are then repackaged and shipped via carrier to the stores. The store needs to sell through those sizes and quantities to you and the consumer.

Shrinkage

Often theft can occur in the supply chain journey. Some drivers may decide to help themselves to a box of clothes from the shipment, causing shrinkage. Shrinkage is an allowance made for lost or stolen goods. This goes into the calculation of demand planning that I mentioned before.

Getting back to the cycle, the clothes have finally made it to the store where they are bought by the consumer. After reviewing the sales data for the shipped items, the logistics cycle adjusts and continues on its way, smoothing out demand spikes, trying to predict what the consumers will want to buy. Every single part of this process is important because money is earned or lost based on these calculations. Do you see how sexy that whole process is? Nothing moves without logistics.

The perception of logistics has come a long way since I was that postgrad going through the newspaper looking for my next opportunity. Fast-forward to the future as companies are seeing what I sensed for years, the crucial contribution that logistics gives to businesses. What's happened in the past has not worked out in the interest of their enterprises. By not fully understanding the total landed cost of products, companies left money on the table.

Companies are now aware that if they want to maximize value, then logistics is something they should invest in. They now see the benefit of researching to find the best supplier, manufacturer, or provider. They've learned that when a product comes in, time is money, and holding on to inventory for any amount of time is costly.

That's why having firm knowledge of demand planning and other elements of the supply chain will dictate consistent availability of inventory. That directive, coupled with ensuring the proper prices of the goods and strategic placement in the marketplace for purchase, ties the whole process together. This is why the entire science of logistics is no longer playing in the background. It's front and center. In this chapter, we'll explore where to place emphasis and attention to ensure effective supply chain logistics presently and in the future.

Overseas versus Country Sourcing: The Endless Debate

I hope I've successfully conveyed the importance of business logistics and how it effectively pushes forward the supply chain. One aspect that is the subject of much debate and deliberation within supply chain rhetoric is outsourcing manufacturing. Most major clothing brands and other product-based companies have opted to cross the ocean for an outsourced manufacturing provider.

Essentially, like every other part of business logistics, it all boils down to cost. The motivating thought behind outsourcing is for companies to take advantage of low production costs so there will be larger margins when the item is sold. Investing next to nothing initially at the stage of creation and getting more back on the back end is a win.

A major example of this was Nike. Nike founder Phil Knight was inspired as a student at Stanford Graduate School of Business to cut costs by outsourcing the manufacturing of his global sneaker brand.[42] The idea from a business point of view was simple: take advantage of the currency rates in another country, and benefit from the higher selling costs in the seller's home country.

It was arbitrage, and it caught on like wildfire. At the time of Nike's creation, a mere 4 percent of US footwear was imported.[43] Presently that same statistic has leaped to 98 percent![44]

---

42   Hayley Peterson, "One Stunning Stat That Shows How Nike Changed the Shoe Industry Forever," Business Insider, accessed February 13, 2024, https://www.businessinsider.com/how-nike-changed-the-shoe-industry-2014-4#:~:text=The%20company's%20founder%2C%20Phil%20Knight,9%25%20of%20its%20manufacturing%20facilities.

43   Peterson, "One Stunning Stat That Shows How Nike Changed the Shoe Industry Forever."

44   Peterson, "One Stunning Stat That Shows How Nike Changed the Shoe Industry Forever."

Nike led this business revolution, causing a lot of companies to enhance their buying power by seeking reduced costs internationally. Companies were rolling along for years reaping the benefits of better costs until they hit a speed bump. What happens to this link of the supply chain when let's say an unprecedented world event occurs, causing the world to shut down? What about when there is catastrophic loss due to a war?

It's a reality that looms over production outsourcing on both ends of the agreement. It could happen in the host company's country, in the outsourced country, or both simultaneously. If an entity is getting all its supplies from one country, that's putting all your eggs in one basket and hoping it doesn't tip over or break any eggs. There are many factors to consider that are often overlooked by the lure of cutting costs. Sure, it may be cheaper in that other country because of labor rates and lower costs, but as it comes to customer service, another huge aspect of the equation, you must be sure that you have a consistent supply readily available.

One way to safeguard this is to diversify your manufacturing base so that you can increase output. That way, if a problem surfaces in one country, then work can be sourced from the alternate country. Another option is to blend your sources with an overseas provider and route some business to stateside suppliers. The benefit of having a blended approach in integrating stateside suppliers is that they don't have the start-up costs or the learning curve that exists when starting up a new manufacturer. This may be a bit costlier because stateside suppliers traditionally cost more, but it is to your benefit to have multiple suppliers readily available. It puts the power in your hands, enabling you to turn the lever on another supplier to increase output to satisfy the production requirements.

Another key benefit to having a supplier in your home country is for strategy. If you want to test out another product line, you don't have to shut down work already in progress or go far away from home. Having a closer supplier allows the flexibility of experimentation and of being on the cutting edge by doing your research and development close to home. Blending your supplier sources is a mutually beneficial arrangement, allowing you to still take advantage of the cheaper international pricing without sacrificing your complete control over output.

Another side to the benefit and ingenuity of outsourcing should be considered. Whenever a company chooses to outsource, it creates a gap in their home country's economy.

Let's use the United States as a case study. When a company shifts and moves production overseas, it creates massive stateside job loss due to the decrease in demand. But as an international shift occurs, like one happening at the time of this book's publication, it disrupts the flow of production and business. Companies are de-risking, or essentially restricting their business, out of China and attempting to get the orders fulfilled here instead.

Currently, the US is experiencing a shortage of workers because manufacturing jobs have been outsourced for multiple decades at this point. Domestic manufacturers have become accustomed to underutilization because outsourcing has been so prevalent for so many years. These de-riskers mistakenly think they can get an order of a billion parts fulfilled here, just as they did at the factories in China. Unfortunately, this country lacks the capacity to produce at the rate that is now in demand. Now to be clear, stateside manufacturing is still a huge contributing factor to the GDP.

In 2023, of the $23.5 trillion earned, manufacturing was the third contributor, adding $2.9 trillion to the country's average.[45] The largest manufacturing subsector in the US is computer and electronic products, followed by chemical manufacturing, then food, beverage, and tobacco products.[46] It's important to mention that this large production of electronics arguably is due in part to the compromised integrity of products and goods being produced in the US, spiking consumerism. If a product is not made with the intention to last, it consistently needs to be replaced, providing work to national factories. In addition to this demand, with nearly a 6 percent decrease in mechanical and electrical manufacturing import business from the US to China, with heavy hitters like Intel, Microsoft, Nike, and Dell pulling out of the East, homegrown manufacturers are guaranteed to see further increases.[47,48]

Having no active workforce to complete the work orders is becoming quite problematic. Stateside parents are not sending their children to school with the expectation of their becoming manufacturing employees, so the workforce is not being replenished. We'll talk more about solutions to combat the diminishing workforce in

45   Govind Bhutada, "Visualizing US GDP by Industry in 2023," Visual Capitalist, accessed February 13, 2024, https://www.visualcapitalist.com/visualizing-u-s-gdp-by-industry-in-2023/.

46   National Institute of Standards and Technology, "US Manufacturing Economy," accessed February 13, 2024. https://www.nist.gov/el/applied-economics-office/manufacturing/manufacturing-economy/total-us-manufacturing#:~:text=The%20largest%20manufacturing%20subsector%20in,2.10%20from%20AMS%20600%2D13.

47   Harry Moser, "Manufacturing Pivots to the United States as Imports from China Plummet," IMTS.com, accessed February 13, 2024, https://www.imts.com/read/article-details/Manufacturing-Pivots-to-the-United-States-as-Imports-from-China-Plummet/1784/type/Read/1.

48   Betsy Atkins. "Manufacturing Moving Out of China for Friendlier Shores," accessed February 13, 2024, https://www.forbes.com/sites/betsyatkins/2023/08/07/manufacturing-moving-out-of-china-for-friendlier-shores/?sh=3f41e08e3541.

the next chapter. For now, I'll state that as manufacturers, we can't ramp up as quickly as the businesses are asking us to because of the lack of stateside investment to replenish the workforce. It becomes a circular movement of increased supply and no workforce to handle the demand. Essentially, there are positive and negative factors in outsourcing and in blending outsourcing with national suppliers. But ultimately the goal is to ensure that each aspect of the supply chain is supported with resiliency and diversity.

Building Resiliency: The Importance of Supply Chain Partnerships

Business is typically a solo game, but not in logistics. As a nation, we're facing some supply chain challenges that could be effectively handled with intentional and strategic partnerships. For a company to become resilient, it's advisable to think outside the box and consider alternative solutions. One solution to increase a company's resiliency is to find a couple of partners willing to invest in smaller companies. By helping them produce greater outputs and fortify their strength with solid partnerships, both companies could grow together. They can build a strong foundational relationship to address demand needs.

For instance, when I was working in corporate America and a supplier partner needed support ramping up to meet our increase in demand, our company would lend it the money to support its growth. It made for good business. That way it didn't have to go to a bank or wait for the long, drawn-out approval process, and it was what a strong strategic partner should do. I think that model should trickle down to manufacturers. It would be mutually beneficial to operate in that capacity. Presently, small and midsized companies, instead of making it easier to do business with companies in need, are increasing payment terms. The terms have increased from net 30 to 45 to 60, and some companies suggest net 120. Then there is an additional expectation that your company also reduce price, even in the face of rising supply and labor costs.

So, if you're a small business trying to maintain your company, now you're acting as a bank, because essentially you're lending the money. If you're getting paid but due to nonadvantageous contractual terms have to wait seventy-five days, how does that help a business that you would want to potentially partner with scale? I contend that it should be the other way around, with more of a consultative approach. It seems as if they want partnership, but at the expense of their partner. On one hand they want client-facing benefits, cutting-edge products, and a high-level of customer service, but at the same time they are degrading the supplier's ability to leverage cash flow to be a stronger partner.

It's a little bit misleading, because the thought process of the supplier is that they want to give us business, but it comes with some costs. Ideally, partnerships can work, but they must be equitable for both parties and beneficial. However, as newspaper cartoonist Johnny Hart said, "Whoever has the gold, makes the rules."[49] The major companies are leveraging their size and strength over their suppliers, but at what cost?

I've been approached by companies that want to give us their manufacturing business, but first they want to cut prices and enter into a longer-term agreement. And they attempt to sell me the dream that this will lead to more business, all under the guise of "partnership." But they are taking a volume approach, which is a bit different.

---

49   Oleg Komlik, "Remember the Golden Rule! Whoever Has the Gold, Makes the Rules!" Economic Sociology & Political Economy, accessed May 28, 2024, https://economicsociology.org/2015/08/28/remember-the-golden-rule-whoever-has-the-gold-makes-the-rules/.

So, counter to a prospective partnership, they expect lower prices, leveraging additional volume. That sounds good in theory only, not in principle. It's hard to scale using that model, especially if you are in custom manufacturing like we are.

I urge small and medium-sized companies to do what I did. Shift your mindset to being open to doing business with companies that value doing business with you. This is important to keep in mind, because in my case of net 30 terms, I still have to pay my supplier within thirty days. I keep in the forefront of my mind a diagram of a graph that illustrates the journey of the net 30 payment term. It begins when the product comes to me and I start the build.

Say that I build it in fifteen days—that still means that in fifteen days I must pay that net 30 bill. In the meantime, my client gets the product on time, as we discussed. Keep in mind that the client's company has proposed a net 75 payment term. So, in seventy-five days, we get paid by the company. That's basically an additional forty-five days I must wait to receive payment. Essentially the money that the client owes to my company can be considered an interest-free loan, while the client has in its possession the finished goods.

The difference lies in the approach between a smaller family-owned business and a major corporation. It's quite apparent in cases of these business dealings. Doing business with a multinational company can be a good thing, but don't go into the situation blindly thinking it will operate as your smaller family-owned business does. Very expensive restrictions will probably be in place for you to do business with it. Bigger companies will have an advantage because of those restrictions. Again, your job as a smaller business is having awareness before entering into partnerships that you believe may benefit your company.

Knowing Your Position within the Supply Chain (Becoming a Good Partner)

As a business owned by a Black woman, we're not necessarily sought out by companies because of my designations. Electro Soft is fortunate to have kept most of the business partnerships it had before I took over the company. The main thing that businesses want assurance on is that you will deliver a top-notch product. Now, don't get me wrong—I get a lot of interest from potential clients who are intrigued by Electro Soft's being Black-owned, but at the end of the day, they want a quality product that is delivered on time.

Additionally, I'm finding that companies are looking to take on triple-bottom-line businesses. Businesses that are all about "the three *p's*"—people, planet, and profit. I'd advise you to consider how your company is making an impact in any way in one of those categories.

A good example is a colleague of mine who has made a commitment to hiring returning citizens, formerly incarcerated individuals. He is satisfying the people category by helping these citizens matriculate back into society by offering stable employment. Additionally, he follows environmental standards by doing his part in contributing to sustainability.

A lot of potential clients are asking to see environmental, social, and governance (ESG) policies, formerly known as CSR (corporate social responsibility). Prospective customers want to see your business as a well-rounded entity that is not just concerned about money. How are you considering the environment in your entity operations, the social component, which includes diversity, and governance of policies that affect your employees and your clientele? It's important to make investments to diversify your company and show potential clients and your community your commitment to serve as well as operate your business. It's a combined effort that will show your dedication to your company.

Potential partners want to know a couple of things. First, that they are doing business with a solid company. Within that, they want to know if the entity can be trusted. Also, how are you impacting your community? So, you'll get asked about your ESG strategy. It's important to diversify your supply chain with diverse companies, such as women- and LGBTQ+-owned businesses in addition to implementing solid ESG practices to help you solidify your business. People want to know who you are, so show them, and help others in the process.

Reflection Points

• **What is your perception of logistics? Are you aware of the process, or do you just have an idea of it?**

Even if you are not the person within your company charged with handling logistics, it will benefit you to understand every part of the link in your supply chain. Back in the day, people would say, "Being foretold is forewarned." In modern speak, that means having a certain cursory knowledge of supply chain logistics will keep you informed and will raise red flags if portions go askew. This way you can attempt to spearhead them with decisive action backed with the right knowledge.

• To outsource or not is truly up to the vision you have for your business.

I mentioned earlier that money is the predominant deciding factor for companies when they seek supply chain partnerships. Saving money is a very valuable part of business solvency, but it's also important to maintain your strategic edge. Putting all your supply eggs in an overseas basket could render some fairly tricky situations to maneuver with your clients. Think about the extended bottom line and not just the now. Your company operates day to day, but for a better future, I urge you to think about the future. Plus, having a homegrown partner within the supply chain can afford a new area of opportunity you may not have considered before.

• To get the best partnerships in logistics, you might want to become a good partner.

You are who you attract. This goes for offshore and partnerships in your native country. Again, money is important to the development of your business, but so is what you add to your community and the people you impact. Think a little bit deeper when it comes to the perception of your business in the national and global marketplace.

CHAPTER SIX

How Do We Attract a Younger Diverse Workforce?

When people can show up as themselves, it's cathartic. Business is about high performance. Allow your workforce to perform at their highest level. As themselves.

—Karla Trotman, CEO of Electro Soft

When I was younger, I was in a popular career development internship program. It was a preparatory program to get college students ready for corporate life. They taught us the skills needed to thrive in the workplace, the way to dress, and other tools essential to fit into the corporate lifestyle. We even learned the virtues of the social aspect of business and were advised to pick up golf. Each student participant hoped to do well so we could intern for four summers at a top company.

The companies that participated weren't shabby either. They were big names that would look amazing on a résumé and provide some powerful experience to assist in furthering a young career. It's amazing how your perception of something changes with knowledge and maturity. Back then I was excited about the new possibilities. If you recall, when I was younger, I desired to dress nicely, go into the city, and have this big, fancy corporate job. This program allowed me to cosplay in my fantasy.

Today, I know that they were teaching us the best way to blend in. You know, the type of blending that causes you to attempt to dress, act, and be like everyone else. Because that was the mission back in the day—not to rock the boat or disrupt the existing environment. That is what we were trained to do at eighteen. No, let me be more direct. We were taught to assimilate. That was in the 1980s and 1990s. Things are a bit different today.

The generations entering adulthood presently, the future of our nation's workforce, are built differently. Generation Z, individuals born between 1997 and 2012,[50] is here and operates unlike any generation before. Here's an example. Antwerp, Belgium, was the host of the 2023 World Artistic Gymnastics Championships. The US men's gymnastics team was there and was being overlooked, as they had been for years. They lost their credibility as a viable contender for the world title in 2014, the last time they claimed a podium spot at the world championship. Little did the team and the world know that this year would prove to be different.

That year, the nineteen-year-old Frederick Richard from Boston, Massachusetts, made his debut championship appearance. The world was familiar with Fred because during the COVID-19 pandemic, like

---

50   Beresford Research, "Age Range by Generation," accessed February 19, 2024, https://www.beresfordresearch.com/age-range-by-generation/.

many from his generation, he garnered national attention from his posts on social media. At the time, the world didn't know that this powerful young Black man would break the nearly decade-long losing streak. He stepped up to do his routine, and it seemed that everyone in the auditorium was holding their breath. He grabbed the high bar and did a flawless routine, nailed his landing, led his team to win it all, and claimed a bronze medal in the all-around category for himself.

The thing that captured my attention, outside his impressive display of athleticism, was the crown of curly, textured twists that were on his head. He was not an image of the decades-past gymnasts who had appeared on this stage before him. His hairstyle, which years ago may have disqualified him at least in part by public and societal judgment, was bravely on display on the world stage, being celebrated with his victory.

Outside his amazing athletic talent, Fred's success was achieved in part because he was allowed to show up as himself. Not to give away the answer to this chapter's opening question so quickly, but to attract a young, thriving, diverse workforce, that is the answer. It's all about stripping away all the old, worn-out, raggedy societal mores that my generation, and those before, had to face.

The list of the usual suspects of discrimination must be buried for us to move forward. The scrutiny of diverse appearances, both in hair and skin tone, and the prejudices that exist systemically should no longer have validity in the future marketplace.

Let's get back to the example with Fred. Imagine if this were a mere ten years ago or anytime before the passing of the federal CROWN Act. This landmark legislation crafted by legal architect D. Wendy Greene makes it constitutionally unethical for states to discriminate against someone with a natural hairstyle like Fred's twists.[51] Had this been a less contemporary time, the athletic prowess displayed by Fred may not have seen the light of day. It's speculative that a coach or some other authority would have demanded he either cut his hair or be deemed ineligible to participate.

Now, in this made-up scenario, we don't know if Fred would have cut his hair or not. It's a good thing it didn't happen that way, and we'll never know. I believe allowing people to show up as themselves in every instance in the workplace will support a diverse workforce. In the next pages, I'll share what I experienced as a young professional, show how detrimental the workforce status quo has been, and illustrate why it needs an overhaul for the sake of national economic stability. Ideally, high-level executives and those separated from the entry-level positions within their industry need only look back at their own entry to be reminded how important inclusion and acceptance are to sustaining a strong, young, and happy workforce.

It's Just Hair, *Right?*

At the end of the last summer of the professional development program, before it was time to officially start my internship, I made the "controversial" decision to get my hair braided into box braids. So that I don't lose anyone, let me describe what the hairstyle entails. *Merriam-Webster* defines box braids as "a section of hair that is parted on the scalp often in a square shape and then braided along its length."

In Black-woman language, box braids are a protective style that gives the hair rest from the rigors of daily styling, featuring individu-

---

51 Nadia Ramlagan, "CROWN Act Would Ban Discrimination Based on Black Hairstyles in Ohio," Public News Service, accessed March 27, 2024, https://www.publicnewsservice.org/2024-01-25/civil-rights/crown-act-would-ban-discrimination-based-on-black-hairstyles-in-ohio/a88431-2.

alized braids of hair from box-shaped parts or sections. For further context, box braids are one of the "controversial" styles that D. Wendy Greene's CROWN Act protects. The style is largely popularized by members of the Black and African diaspora. They are so prevalent presently that people barely blink an eye at seeing a professional Black woman with box braids. But back in the day, that was *not* the case!

My decision to get box braids was a risky one at the time. It was worth it to me, though, because I wanted to express myself and my individuality. On the other hand, it was counter to the corporate culture staple, straight hair, which I learned was acceptable in the internship program. When it was time for me to start my internship at my chosen company, it caused me great anxiety. To be clear, neither the internship program nor the company I worked for said or did anything directly to make me feel that way. It was the secret understanding that I couldn't really wear my hair the way I wanted to. The way I wanted to wear it didn't fit with the image I'd been taught. My braids were professional, but I didn't want to draw any attention to myself for being different from the rest of the other interns. And even though I felt the anxiety, I did it anyway.

The ironic thing was, I didn't feel like myself while wearing those braids. I felt that although I was showing up as myself, I felt like a stranger doing it—unlike the alternate version of myself who dressed up, trying hard to align with the business status quo. By showing up as myself, I wasn't confident that it was OK, because it was counter to what we were trained to do. But again, all these feelings arose from hair. Not my attendance, job performance, or other metrics. It was *hair*!

I felt like an anarchist for choosing to express myself naturally. My parents were in disbelief that I would wear braids to the company for work even though they were freshly done, pulled back, and neat.

And although no one from the company said anything to me when I was working, their body language at times would speak volumes.

That's the thing about discrimination. Its presence is so stifling that it is easily recognizable when it enters the room. As I remember that experience, it's probably also where I created the duality of my speaking voice. Back then we didn't have the language to define it, but now, switching the way you naturally speak to assimilate to your environment is called code-switching. Think of a professional manner of speaking on steroids. It's not just simply using the right diction and pronunciation of words and avoiding excessive colloquialism. No, it's something worse. It is speaking in different phrasing and using terms aligned with the dominant culture in a given work environment. It's knowing who you are but being forced to speak in a particular language to fit in. I had been code-switching for so long in my career, not realizing it had been culturally ingrained. While I do believe that I have the freedom to say the things I want and express myself in my own voice, I recognize that for economic survival, you do what you have to do.

After college, thankfully, this switched up a bit when I started working for companies that were more liberal. It seems in a lot of ways they allowed people to express themselves. A good example of this freedom was when I worked at the Swedish furniture store, IKEA. IKEA's staff was as unique as the company's name. You'd see people with different-colored hair, piercings, and tattoos work their way from the sales floor up the ranks of the company's organizational structure to management and sometimes the corporate level.

In fact, because of their comfort with tattoos, they were celebrated, and sometimes some of the team members would get IKEA tattoos! These loyal employees would be featured in ad campaigns and get other recognition. That's how I saw firsthand the power of inclusion in the workplace. Now, from the outside looking in, companies from my past would not have been cool with the free culture that IKEA had cultivated. But it was all good, because dominant culture had always dictated what professionalism looked like. IKEA ran counter to the tired narrative.

My time at IKEA shaped my perception of individualism in the workplace. It's something that I've brought with me to my company. My two brothers, who've worked in different capacities in the company, express themselves with piercings and by locking their hair. Individuality is a driving force in the culture of Electro Soft. I remember interviewing an impressive young lady in her twenties for a role on our team. At the end of the great conversation, she hesitantly mentioned she had a question. She then asked if it was OK that she had green hair and tattoos. My response was simple: I didn't care what color her hair was, as long as she showed up and did a good job. She smiled in relief, as she, too, had faced forced conformity in other jobs in the past.

It's always been my experience that people show up when they are allowed to be themselves authentically. It makes for a more productive environment. When authenticity is not a staple in the culture, it places an emotional toll on your team. Studies have shown that authenticity is a favorable state for employees, reducing strain, enhancing job performance and satisfaction, and promoting lower turnover.[52] In my opinion, as humans, we truly want to be accepted for who we are. Any company that is willing to embrace a person's full self will get in return that person's full potential.

---

52 Anne Sutton and Madeleine Stapleton, "When It's Not Safe to Be Me: Employee Authenticity Mediates the Effect of Perceived Manager Psychopathy on Employee Well-Being," BMC Psychology, October 9, 2023, accessed February 9, 2024, https://bmcpsychology.biomedcentral.com/articles/10.1186/s40359-023-01333-w.

Based on my experiences at the beginning of my career, I realized there's freedom in being yourself in the environment in which you earn your living. I've shared this with my management team. People are different, some leaning toward the conservative side and others being more liberal. I insist they view our company as I do America, as a salad with a healthy variety of individual ingredients all contributing to the bowl.[53] I know everyone says America is a melting pot, but it's now time for a new approach. Something fresher, healthier, and equally delicious: acceptance of authenticity.

Meeting Young Workers Halfway

Getting young workers to work in manufacturing is … well, it's hard. It all comes down to conditioning. As I mentioned when we first began this journey in chapter 1, it's not the younger generation that I must convince about the virtues of working in manufacturing. Once they come into the factory and see the unique opportunity and the work we offer, they get interested. They curiously anticipate an opportunity to try something new and different from the generations that preceded them. The issue that arises is convincing their parents to break through the archaic school-to-college blueprint that has been followed for years.

But the reality is that parents don't care if their children have an interest in something other than the college track. It's not something they want to entertain. The truth is that after graduation, young people want to do different things. In the fourth quarter of 2023,

---

53   Bruce Thornton. "Melting Pots and Salad Bowls: What Is the Future of Assimila-
tion in America?" Hoover Institution, accessed May 28, 2024, https://www.hoover.
org/research/melting-pots-and-salad-bowls#:~:text=Starting%20in%20the%20
1960s%2C%20however,of%20law%20and%20the%20market.

Business Insider published an online article stating that "Gen Z is the new threat to the American College Experience.[54]" That's major.

In a study conducted by Business Insider and YouGov, 46 percent of Gen Zers surveyed felt that it's counterintuitive to put themselves in debt to further understand educational concepts they learned in their primary education.[55] They find it far more beneficial to take the road less traveled without higher education and either take up a trade or become their own boss via entrepreneurship. For a lot of them, because of the cost of higher education, they are starting to view it as a sham.

This shift in thought process shows a trend that could benefit industries that have been overlooked, like manufacturing. It seems that this younger generation is ready to do away with the old limiting career pathways of the past and is putting their own interests first. That is where barrier industries can step in and meet interested young workers halfway.

To do that, a couple of things need to happen: number one is accessibility. We've gone over going out into the community and having a presence for young workers to see. But there is a need to discuss the opposite. What if there is interest from Gen Z, but they have a barrier keeping them from a potential debt-free career choice? Let me be specific. I have a son who is a Gen Zer, and like most parents, I found myself asking him what he wanted to do with his future. He told me that he and two of his friends were going to get a place locally and go to school. I encouraged him to not be limited to his hometown, but I told him I would support his plans.

---

54   Ayelet Sheffey, "Gen Z Is the New Threat to the American College Experience," Business Insider, December 23, 2023, accessed February 19, 2024.

55   Sheffey, "Gen Z Is the New Threat."

Then I considered his two friends' paths. I figured since my son was making plans with them, their career trajectory should be on my radar as much as his. One of them was closer in age to my son, and the other was slightly older and would be graduating soon. Fast-forward to one year later, and the oldest student has indeed graduated, but his plans have shifted a bit. He's not enrolled in college and is working at a local restaurant, living at home with his mother. I had my husband connect with his family to inquire if he had an interest in electronics. If so, Electro Soft had an opportunity for him. He'd have to find his way to us because we are located in the suburbs, outside Philadelphia where he lives.

What he did next shows that connecting with a young person with the desire to succeed and giving them a chance is beneficial for everyone involved. This young man who didn't have a car researched how he could get to Electro Soft and mapped out a route using public transportation. To get to us, his potential employer, he would have to take two trains and a bus and then walk a mile. He accepted the challenge because it gave him an opportunity, something that wasn't being offered at his part-time employer. Not to mention, he was also interested in electronics. That type of determinism and fire is what drives this younger generation. So, he is presently taking advantage of an opportunity that allows him to work forty hours a week where he can learn more about something in which he is interested.

Do you see how that old dynamic has shifted? Instead of going to a higher-learning institution and paying for the knowledge and hoping for a job afterward, this young man is getting paid to learn skills and a career path. I remember when I told him that I would hire him, he was so excited! Before he left his interview, I had to ask him how he planned on handling the commute. He said he'd get up at 2:30 a.m. and would make it happen. I was shocked but realized it was not for me to question his desire and ability. The mother in me had so many objections, but I realized he was fueled by something stronger—a desire for something better. We've taken him on, and he is a part of the team. This young man is making the effort that exists from his desire for a better future; the least I could do is to meet him halfway.

Along the same lines, a young lady was referred to me as a mentee by a woman I knew locally. This young lady also had potential aspirations to go to college, but her plans changed. Again, I asked her, as I asked my son's friend, if she had any interest in manufacturing. She did, and we onboarded her through a program our county created for young adults aged eighteen to twenty-five looking for paid work experience. She got knowledge, and I got a new employee. I pose a question to the founders and business owners reading my words right now: "What are you willing to invest to meet this younger generation halfway?"

Some of them will be like my son's friend, willing to get to work by any means necessary to secure a brighter future. Will you receive them, or will you present more barriers for them by blocking their opportunities? That is what I feel about this younger workforce. They have learned from the generations that have preceded them, and they don't want to be swallowed by a mountain of debt from their education. If nurtured properly, this is an opportunity to handpick the next generation of sharp, intelligent minds who want more for their lives. We should give it to them.

Another key point to recruiting an active youthful workforce is to understand and provide what they want. Just as the mindset of the younger generation is different, so are their wants and needs. For example, the must-have job benefits for the baby boomer generation consist of good healthcare benefits, including vision, medical, and dental as well as life insurance, financial counseling, and employer match for 401(k)s.[56]

Gen Zers want a completely different type of benefits package, more on the holistic level. After seeing the world shut down in 2020 due to the global pandemic, they want a sure thing with their employment. Their list of wants includes tuition reimbursement, flexible paid time off, a hybrid or remote work environment, mental and physical healthcare, and employee assistance programs (EAPs).[57] Gen Z wants the freedom of choice and flexibility and not to feel controlled by their place of employment.

As it relates to entry-level manufacturing, remote work is not possible because it's floor work, but we can make the environment appealing mentally and with a liberal culture, as mentioned before. To attract the workers you want, you must give them what they want, within reason. A problem we've noticed with the younger generation is their attachment to their phones, which distracts them from the tasks they are doing, and it's a safety hazard. We have to stress to them that even if they're working on a ten-dollar wire, that wire will go into a million-dollar product, so it's important to pay attention. Typically after that interaction, they might feel some sort of way and decide this environment is not for them and quit.

This generation was born at the height of the technological era, which correlates with limited attention spans. That being understood, job descriptions should include attention as one of the leading qualifiers, as it is now becoming a skill. After the cell phone–dependent talent made their exit from Electro Soft, I made the executive decision to work with programs looking to place young adults in paid work

56 Leap Carpenter Kemp Insurance Agency, "The Most Important Employee Benefits by Generation," accessed February 20, 2024, https://www.lckinsurance.com/blog/employee-benefits/most-important-employee-benefits-by-generation.

57 Leap Carpenter Kemp, "The Most Important Employee Benefits by Generation."

experiences. I found that students trained in those programs make solid transitions into full-time work. From there, I pulled together school administrators, teachers, county officials, and those training youth to see how we could successfully onboard more young people.

A Formulaic Approach: Creating a Combined Culture with Multiethnicities

Philadelphia, like many parts of America, is a haven of racial and ethnic diversity. Its Asian residents make up nearly 8 percent of its population.[58] At Electro Soft, we're grateful to be a company that employs a diverse range of employees. A lot of our team is originally from Cambodia and Vietnam. A unique challenge of having a multiethnic team is discovering how to onboard and support diverse employees without having segregated groups within the overall community of the company.

As a Black female CEO, I understand. When you get hired in a new role, you form an affinity group, whether it's informal or formal. Although Black professionals fit into the work aspect of a role, we're accustomed to not readily fitting into the social company culture. We naturally form relationships with our fellow employees and colleagues who look like us. I think it occurs because there is a part of us we don't get to bring to work. We then find comfort in others who understand where we're coming from without having to be told.

At Electro Soft, we're actively working to shape our overall culture to ensure that it is inclusive for all. Our main core values—presence, team, and pride—are the driving forces for creating our culture,

---

58   Data USA: Philadelphia, PA, accessed February 19, 2023, https://datausa.io/
      profile/geo/philadelphia-pa/#:~:text=The%205%20largest%20ethnic%20
      groups,(Hispanic)%20(4.69%25).

along with a formulaic approach to achieve this. As an example, for a majority of our Asian team, English is their second language, so we are working to onboard a Vietnamese and a Khmer-speaking professional to train our immigrant employees.

Having a strong, solid onboarding process is imperative. Sixty-nine percent of employees are more likely to stay with a company for a minimum of three years if they have a good onboarding process.[59] That is what we want to achieve. A satisfied, properly onboarded staff for our native employees as well as our immigrants. The goal is for them to ease their transition seamlessly into an English-speaking environment.

Again, as I've urged you to do when hiring younger talent, the same applies to diverse talent. Some of the team members from Asia have said that in the past they worked in nail shops and didn't like the smell of the chemicals or the long hours working on the weekends. Some of the roles they worked in the past didn't offer any benefits, had inconsistent work hours, and were also cash-only environments.

Without proper payroll records, they would get paid without pay stubs. Without verifiable income, they weren't able to buy homes. In manufacturing, we offer them steady paychecks and are working to have an on-call Realtor to assist them in finding their first home. We want them to feel they are equipped with a professional who can help them understand the way their credit scores work, etc. We gladly give them what they want because the US is in a labor drought that spans industries.

Not to keep citing the pandemic as the source of all the woes in manufacturing, but factually, 1.4 million jobs were lost, and we have

---

59   Tim Newham, "26 Surprising Onboarding Statistics for 2024," Think-Learning.com, accessed February 20, 2024, https://www.think-learning.com/onboarding/onboarding-statistics/#:~:text=69%25%20of%20employees%20are%20more,them%20stay%20at%20the%20job.

had difficulties rebounding ever since.[60] Not to be too bleak, because a resurgence is trending, but there are still 616,000 total manufacturing job openings that need filling.[61] With numbers like that, it's a major power play to create an environment to incentivize workers to not only want to work for you but to stick around. And if you take your time and nurture new hires, they will refer their friends and other members of their community to you.

Keep in mind, another issue we have is transportation, as we are not located in the city, but having groups of individuals who are from the same community and live near each other enables them to carpool into work together. Just a cautionary note: if you hire family members, they will come together, and conversely, they won't come to work together. If one of them were to get sick or disgruntled, you run the risk of none of them coming or their not being content at work. You have to handle these situations cautiously and professionally to protect the privacy of all parties involved.

Another major part of our formula is to give high-quality training to our staff, so they understand that an opportunity for growth exists. Hardly ever does someone want to be on a job or in a role where they know there is no possibility for them to expand. We have a stair-step model that we've rolled out, showing them the skills or certification it takes to get to the next level. It's helpful to get them excited and looking forward to the future. It's good for them to see the advancement rather than just hear about it.

---

60 Stephanie Ferguson and Makinizi Hoover. "Understanding America's Labor Shortage: The Most Impacted Industries," accessed February 20, 2024, https://www.uschamber.com/workforce/understanding-americas-labor-shortage-the-most-impacted-industries.

61 Ferguson and Hoover, "Understanding America's Labor Shortage."

Reflection Points

• **Acceptance and appreciation for employee authenticity will create a strong, secure, sustainable youthful workforce.**

That allowance of entering an environment as yourself is liberating. And even to this day, although I can wear my hair however I want to wear it, I think about how I was the rogue ambassador wearing my hair in braids on day one of my internship. I feel like it's still my job and duty to show up with strength so that young folks and other team members understand that two things can exist at the same time. You can still be professional and show up the way your hair grows out of your head, among other innate traits. Founders and CEOs with an internal commitment to creating company cultures that accept employees as they are will undoubtedly notice an increase in productivity and happiness within their business.

• **The emerging workforce is different; be prepared to meet them where they are at.**

They are not playing ball with the old, raggedy, school-to-college, student loan debt, working-for-a-meager-wage educational structure. They want something different that generations before them seemingly didn't have—freedom. It's our role, if we want a satisfied and thriving workforce, to meet them in the middle and provide opportunities that engage and excite them. No one, regardless of their age or status in life, wants to feel as if they're stuck. In liberating the old work model, we open ourselves to a new opportunity to do things a better way. What will you choose?

- **To get a young reliable workforce, make your company appealing for them to work with.**

Gen Zers have seen from the millennials and Gen Xers how debt from higher education weighs them down, keeping them stuck working in an unfulfilling job and making wages below their talents. They want to feel a sense of freedom and to work in an environment that nurtures their individuality. Understand this, and you'll get a solid workforce. Also, hire a staffing professional to recruit for you. They can sense things about a candidate that you may miss in your eagerness to fill a role. Trust me, I've been there. The investment of hiring an agency will save your company time and effort.

- **Embrace the diversity of your workforce.**

Embracing the diversity of your workforce is not something that involves a twelve-tiered DEI program laminate on the wall. It's quite simple—getting down to what your team needs and supplying it. If they need consistent hours so they can plan their personal time effectively, give it to them. If they need a snapshot of potential career development, provide it to them. Just as you service your clients and customers by providing a solution for their issues, do the same for your teammates. A happy team is a team that stays and tells others about you and the environment you've cultivated.

CHAPTER SEVEN

How Do We Deliver Value to Our Customers?

Serving your customer to the highest level is letting them know that you are an extension of their company. This builds a level of comfort that is unparalleled. People do business with people, not just the company.

—Karla Trotman, CEO of Electro Soft

Customer service, also known as customer or client experience, is a huge component of any thriving business. Ironically, it seems as if companies are treating customer service as an afterthought, an archaic relic. Without customer satisfaction, you have no company. I don't know if it's the advancement of modern technology that has made customer service slip in the ranking of operational priorities, but I think it's time to implement traditional concepts when it comes to nurturing client and customer relationships.

Sometimes you have to get up from behind the keyboard, put the phone down, and go to the client. Make that personal connection. Let them see the expression on your face, shake your hand, and feel your sincerity. I'd like to share with you our formula for doing that. Before I do, I want to affirm that this chapter isn't meant to be preachy, but I do want to emphasize how vitally and crucially important it is to serve your clients and customers. Also, your company may not be able to do in-person visits. That is understandable depending on the nature of your business. As we review our formula, you may choose to personalize this for your business. Think about how this would work for your business model and structure.

A lot of our customers are within driving distance of our facility, which includes one of our larger customers. To provide context on our initial client operations, our customers don't forecast the work they request of us. Once we provide them a quote on what their work projects entail, we don't know exactly when we're getting the project. It tends to show up unexpectedly via a purchase order. And in turn, the client's expectation is that we will be able to fill that order within the time frame. There is no problem with that, but if we are in progress on another order or if simultaneously another job comes through at the same time, the timeline needs to be adjusted a bit. Every client wants to be a priority, but with the reality of the workforce drought issues, a bit of maneuvering on our part is required.

So, in the case of one of our largest clients, we had a scenario very similar to the one described. This is how we solved the issue. This particular client had been doing business with us for years, but there had been a slight hiatus in their orders with us. This is not an uncommon occurrence in our business. Remember how we covered the benefits of having a diversified manufacturing supply chain in your business structure? Well, here is an example of what it looks like on the consumer end. Our client must have outsourced the work to another manufacturer for its projects. One day, they returned to us without any notice to fill a work order for hundreds of thousands of US dollars of work. It was several months of work that we weren't expecting. And they wanted us to do it on a relatively tight timeline.

Technically, we couldn't fulfill the order. However, as a longer-term client, they were worth the effort. We strive to go above and beyond to accommodate and help return business. We took on the order even though we knew it would put us in a difficult position. Also, it should be mentioned that at the time, we had a lot of new people getting acclimated to their roles, and we were onboarding them. It was the perfect storm.

Then on top of it all, the client's priorities shifted, causing a change in the scope of work. The situation was that we had already ordered all the materials for the initial project as described by the client. It had been shipped priority, and since we'd paid for it, we had to shelve the materials because we did not need them immediately. The materials for the original latter part of the project we did need immediately because the project had changed, causing us to scramble to get what we needed to fulfill the order.

After that, a back-and-forth email exchange regarding the project ensued. Electro Soft and the client finally got on the same page, and we got to work and finished a portion of the company's order. Typically, we ship every product order and do not hand deliver them. But I knew that our typical service was not going to cut it in this instance. So, we pushed out all the finished products we had at the time and loaded them up in my car, along with some little treats for everyone. My goal was for them to feel heard and for me to convey that we appreciated their business.

When I got there, I told them we were both frustrated, and I provided a solution for us to get to a happier place. I suggested they tell us what their top priority was and then give us their second-tier priority. It was a simple conversation. There was no yelling, just two businesses discussing their frustrations and moving toward solutions. My presence let them know we wanted to make them happy, and we were able to work out the issue face-to-face.

That is the first tenet of our formulaic customer service approach—upholding the crucial component, communication. Nearly all missteps in both business and personal life occur due to a breakdown or misunderstanding of expectations. Outside the skills that you have to cultivate for the day-to-day operations of your business, the next most important asset is to have clear, solid, and strong communication.

Communication Is Crucial

Now, in the example with my long-term client, we could have stayed on an email chain until forever. However, modern technological communication embodies some risks. Sometimes many people are carbon copied, or cc'd, on the email who are not essential to the situation, and their input convolutes the message. This communication confusion can be costly for all parties involved. Fifty-five percent of companies use email when communicating with their clients, and 12 percent have lost customers to competitors due to communication issues.[62]

Email is important in business interactions, but it does increase the margin of error. Reduce the margin of error by taking a bigger role in the communication and getting face to face with the client. We've found it to be so helpful. My father taught me this personal touch a

---

62   "Communication Statistics 2024," Project.co, accessed February 23, 2024, https://
     www.project.co/communication-statistics/.

long time ago. I'm sure the way I handled the situation with our client was how he would have done it had he still been running the company.

To that point, as the CEO of a company, a solid leadership stance will help impact your client interaction. Leadership is highly demonstrative, and if you are a good leader, the way you handle breakdowns of communication will impress upon your staff the importance of a client-first model. My hand delivering the partial order communicates to my team that I am willing to step in at some of the most uncomfortable and highly stressful times to ensure that our clients are well taken care of. I could have easily continued the email thread with our client or called their contact on the phone. But when I stopped by, they were surprised to see me, and it made an impression. That lets both employees and clients know that the leader of the company cares.

To be honest, I'd have it no other way. This is how it should be. With the nature of my business, I see companies outsourcing work to other countries for cheaper production costs daily. I make it a priority to be dedicated to making our business interactions work. I truly honor everyone who does business with Electro Soft, and I want them to feel it.

Another way that makes an impact with communication efforts is by having an open door—or in our case an "open factory"—policy that we extend to all our clients. Typically when constructing an order for a client, we get the drawings and schematics sent directly to us. At Electro Soft we have four different areas designated for different electronics assembly needs: printed circuit boards, cables, wire harnesses (which are essentially complex cable assemblies), and box builds/enclosures.

We don't manufacture bare printed circuit boards (PCBs); we build component assemblies according to our customers' assembly prints and schematics. The value we provide to our many customers over the years is our ability to interpret their drawings and understand them. At times everything that is put on paper doesn't always translate well into production, and we've found that a lot of issues can arise during this phase. To spearhead that, we've found it beneficial to have closer relationships with the engineers who work with us. We're able to either go to their facility or they come to ours, or we do a video chat to discuss the issues we're having. And we don't wait. Without hesitation we seek clarity, because what we sell is time. Communication is something that we do proudly.

It's an honor to have the strong relationships we've developed over the years with the engineers. We will drop off the finished product, or just stop at their company to see if there are any issues or if there's anything we're missing. The fortunate thing is that this relationship is reciprocal. They feel comfortable enough coming over to us and dropping in if they have an issue … or just to say "Hi."

We always tell our customers that because we're an extension of their manufacturing facility, they have the freedom to drop in at any time and don't need to make an appointment. That's a liberty you can have when your operational activities are consistent. There's nothing we would be doing differently during the workday whether they are there or not. Since they realize we do have other customers as well, they recognize that we may not be working on a particular project that they own. We find it's a big value add in the high-level comfortability of not only knowing who's working on your product but also knowing their experience level. This level of comfort allows the development of the collaborative aspect of partnership to be visible.

There's a benefit when you work closely together. Over the years we have picked up the design nuances of the design engineers who create the products we build. When we take a drawing from on paper to build, working out issues becomes easier as the years wear on, which allows for faster resolution. This builds an intuitive relationship where the client is aware of what we're doing, and it makes it easier to recognize any incidents as they occur. This allows the ability to work through issues a little bit more fluidly. It clears up any opportunities for any miscommunication or issues that could occur without familiarity. That's what they want—a consultative partner to make it less robotic.

When building custom electronics, you're creating a small piece that will go into the whole of something else. Making mistakes or errors while configuring all those parts is highly dangerous, so it's crucial to ensure the people assembling from the print understand what the engineer had in mind. This collaboration and exchange of knowledge to create a product or correct an issue is, in my opinion, the new wave of customer service. Interaction with your customers will take you further than having a hands-off relationship with them.

Don't take it just from my experiences. The numbers don't lie: 73 percent of consumers will switch to a competitor after they have bad experiences with an existing company they're doing business with.[63] As it relates to customer collaboration, customer-first operations can yield up to a 700 percent return on investment over twelve years.[64] And here's one more to consider—77 percent of business owners and leaders realize that securing a personal relationship with clients leads to retaining more customers.[65]

Now that empirical and concrete evidence has been presented, delivering customer service to your clients is achievable by knowing which relationships to nurture within the company, retaining those relationships, mitigating costs for the clients, and still providing

---

63   Court Bishop, "51 Customer Service Statistics You Need to Know," Zendesk.com, last updated February 13, 2024, accessed February 21, 2024, https://www.zendesk.com/blog/customer-service-statistics/.

64   Bishop, "51 Customer Service Statistics."

65   Bishop, "51 Customer Service Statistics."

optimal service through labor shortages. As we continue, keep in mind that the goal of this chapter is to provide actionable solutions to ensure that you serve your customers or clients to the highest degree possible. Taking care of them should yield a profitable outcome for your business and a revenue stream that will replenish itself with your dedicated commitment to client-first service.

Mitigating Production Costs

Here is a bit of information you may or may not know: people go into business for the profit of it all. If they didn't want this major element, then they'd be working predominantly in charity. This is a tongue-in-cheek way to introduce profit margins into the conversation. Another huge foundational piece of customer service is to lower production costs and subsequently risks for clients. The way you do that is to win in business by getting all your final costs as small as possible.

Electro Soft works with a variety of different customers. About 90 percent of our business is from the private sector in commercial and industrial, and 10 percent is from the public sector by way of government contracts. Across the board, they all want costs that are affordable and can yield a high return. They opt to do business with us because we offer them a consistent level of quality at a specific price. This is a major part of our business. If a company were to do manufacturing in-house yet not do it frequently, it would be hard for them to have a consistent labor rate, and they would ultimately lose money.

In other cases, some companies have in-house manufacturing, and they've had a surge in orders. So, they need an assist. We'll then take on an aspect of their manufacturing to help lighten their workload. In either case, the value that we bring is flexibility and providing them with an option to mitigate their costs and efforts.

You may be thinking, *After we just went over an entire chapter on outsourcing, how is it possible for us to have business at the rate that we do?* What we didn't discuss earlier was some of the other less-considered factors of *outsourcing* that can hinder a business. When people hear the term *outsourcing*, they automatically think of the costs saved by doing business with companies based internationally. But they don't consider some of the other societal ramifications that could hurt a company's image if consumers knew about them. Specifically, think of the governance piece that we discussed earlier.

As a reminder, companies want to do business with other companies that they know are making a difference in their communities, uplifting them, providing opportunities, and other positive outcomes. However, those are our country's internal standards. One huge component that companies need to keep in mind is the child labor laws and how they're different from the US laws. What is commonplace in another culture may be cause for concern here stateside.

Another thing to consider is the adult workers who work in these factories. Are they working under forced labor and in an environment with unsafe conditions? Do they have access to drinking water on site and are given bathroom breaks? Are they forced to work overtime? Is the factory hazardous without air-conditioning, ventilation, or fans?

There is no guarantee. Of course, someone may go to do on-site visits, but sometimes those things are not considered. Think of it this way. There is a business-to-business model and a business-to-consumer model. So, a consumer product—like a refrigerator, for example—is an item sold to a major retailer like the electronics store Best Buy. Ultimately it will go into a consumer's home. So, if the consumer follows the outsourcing component of the supply chain and perhaps becomes aware that the products were made in overseas factories by enslaved children, that's an issue.

People vote with their dollars and protest by deciding not to buy products made in less-than-favorable conditions. The issue becomes a bit different in the business-to-business model. If a company is making a product that goes into an industrial environment, typically they are not aware if it has been made by a factory using child labor. Unfortunately, people don't think that far up in the value chain in that way because it's not as visible. But it is still a concern companies should care about.

This dedicated concern around ethics and environmental factors causes business-to-business companies like Electro Soft to have an edge. Remember, a client can drop by our factory any day they'd like. They have the comfort of knowing personally whom they are doing business with and can observe our team and see that our people are happy. Our team's happiness is how we deliver optimal service.

As you read the heading for this section, I'm sure your mind went to dollars and cents being the only cost to mitigate. It is important, but there is another cost to consider as it relates to upholding your client's business. Specifically, what is a company willing to give up to have a short-term gain? It's cheap on one end but costly on the other. Nobody wants negative press, but they do want to know, hopefully, that their business dealings are solid. At the end of the day, the financial health of the firm is at the top of the list.

Nurturing and Retaining Key Relationships

Of the 90 percent of customers we serve in the private sector, 95 percent are repeat business. One of our clients has been in business with us for over twenty-five years. We've kept them with a collaborative and consultative approach. We know the individuals we work with the most on their projects and nurture those relationships. We actively communicate with all the design engineers and ask specific questions in the midst of their building the project. We leave the communication pathway open and active.

This means asking if there is a problem on either end. We jointly and actively resolve the issue. We've also always had a really good relationship with the buyers. Buyers are an important part of the process because they hold the purchasing power of the company. They may not know every aspect of the project they're buying for, so we make it easy for them by explaining what they're buying and fielding any questions or concerns they have about cost. Taking that time to inform them by using layman's terms makes it a lot easier for all parties involved.

For example, sometimes it makes more cost-effective sense to buy a package of four of an item rather than a single quantity of the item due to packaging unit costs. Once they get the explanation, they feel comfortable moving forward because we've shown the benefits to them and have successfully established trust. And I think sometimes people underestimate how valuable it is to become a trusted source to your clients. Established trusting relationships were helpful as the company transitioned from my father to me. And even though buyers for a company may move on, often we still maintain a relationship with the initial buyer Electro Soft worked with, which often turns into new business at a new company.

At one particular company, even though the original buyer my father worked with has retired, she's still in touch. She and my father have become friends over the years, and she knew my mother. Subsequent buyers who have worked there after her have also established relationships with us. I can't stress the importance of relationship building with key decision-makers within your client's company structure. Those foundational relationships can help minimize risk and maintain their bottom line as well as increase yours.

That is the part of our relationship we are responsible for. They have a lot of things coming down the pipeline, and focusing on the manufacturing aspect of that project shouldn't be one of them. They should be able to do what they do confidently knowing that we are holding our portion down. That is the ultimate goal—to instill confidence in our clients. Our greatest compliment is to be an asset to our clients by delivering value in every aspect of interaction.

Reflection Points

• Customer service may seem like it's in the intensive care unit, but by reinstilling old-school virtues, it can be nurtured and brought back to life.

In 2022, when businesses were wrecked by the global shutdown, the major corporations that were thriving were those that took care of their clients with a client-first approach. Whether it was consumers or other businesses, having a client-first approach ensured sustainability. I invite you to take a nonjudgmental look at your customer relationships. Do your clients feel that they are the priority in your business model? What improvements, if any, could you make?

• Think back to your most recent interaction with a client. Did it go well? If not, it may be time to revisit your communication directives and policies within the company.

So many things can go askew in business. It's best to improve your communication, or you run the risk of it becoming a failing aspect. Maybe that means instead of having a phone call or an email exchange, it might be time to go to the client if you're able or do a videoconference. Sometimes it's best to handle business face-to-face to make sure everyone is on the same page to eliminate any confusion or missteps in communication. Technology's innovation is a gift to our society. But the traditional aspect of communication, face-to-face communication, shouldn't be taken for granted. Use it to bridge a better channel of verbal homogeny between you and your clients.

• **How can you lighten the load for your clients?**

One of the best ways to do that is to ensure that your business operations are tight. Money is a huge component of business for sure, but there are also other ways to gain profit and revenue and conversely lose it as well. By considering and securing various aspects of your business operations, you ensure that your relationship with every client is solid. Again, companies don't necessarily just do business with companies; they do business with people.

• **Prioritize building strong relationships with both new and long-term clients.**

To have clients who have done business with us for over twenty-five years is truly a blessing. One of the ways we ensure they stay with us and that they're happy with us is that we prioritize establishing and maintaining relationships with key roles within their company infrastructure. Although the relationships exist through business, they aren't completely all about business. We facilitate a relationship with our clients, both new and old, in which they feel they can trust us, are heard, and trust the needs of their business will be fulfilled. Think about the day-to-day operations in your company. How can you strengthen the relationships of the key individuals you deal with in your business operations from other companies?

CHAPTER EIGHT

How Do We Build Noncompetitive Industry Partnerships?

If you want to go fast, go alone. If you want to go far, go together.

—African Proverb

One of the curious by-products of being in business is the inevitable possibility of competition. It's as if businesspeople automatically feel they are in some great race to be "the best." Business is a game, no doubt, but there is seldom only one winner. What they're experiencing is a spirit of scarcity as opposed to abundance. A scarcity mindset can detract from any business environment. It's a belief system that is rooted in fear and anxiety, often leading to competitive actions.[66]

---

66 Lizzie Benton, "The Silent Threat of Scarcity Mindset in the Workplace," Liberty Mind, accessed April 2, 2024, https://libertymind.co.uk/the-silent-threat-of-scarcity-mindset-in-the-workplace/#:~:text=The%20scarcity%20mindset%2C%20as%20the,and%20self%2Ddefeating%20work%20environment.

Working in business sometimes dictates a tendency to be very insular, causing us to focus only on what is right in front of us. We work with our heads down, constantly in motion, putting out fires, getting the right people on our teams, and handling other concerns. Sometimes we forget that the challenges we face are not brand new. Others have seen them and gotten past them before. We need to pick our heads up from our day-to-day and connect with others in our industry and adjacent industries to facilitate the brilliance of business to arise.

The solution is creating strategic industry partnerships, a multi-employer collaborative effort that brings together management and labor around common purposes.[67] The truth is that partnerships, done effectively, can strengthen the bottom lines of all businesses involved and positively affect their consumers. Regardless of your industry, there are always viable opportunities to fortify partnerships.

A good case study of this is Amazon, the online shopping behemoth. From its independent retail sellers to contract manufacturers, it understands the concept of partnership. Its private label strategy, with offerings like AmazonBasics, has quickly become popularized and used at scale by consumers.[68] Its relationships with manufacturing partners allow it to cast a wider net and reach a larger market, demonstrating the immense benefit of partnerships.

Then there's Uber and Spotify. At a glance, it may seem like these two brands might not have that much in common. Spotify is an online music and media streaming app, and Uber is a transporta-

---

67   Philadelphia Works, "The Southeastern Pennsylvania Manufacturing Alliance," accessed April 5, 2024, https://philaworks.org/business-solutions/industry-partnerships/sepma/.

68   Hale Cosmeceuticals, Inc., "Contract Manufacturing and Brand Success: Strategies for Collaboration," accessed April 4, 2024, https://www.halecosmeceuticals.com/blog/contract-manufacturing-and-brand-success-strategies-for-collaboration.

tion service. However, these two companies entered a partnership to create "a soundtrack for your ride," enabling passengers to choose the music playing during their trip.[69] They are both getting engagement from their users and staying relevant. It's a win-win for both companies—that is the goal.

What I've found with Electro Soft is that there is power in having industry partnerships. There is a benefit in relating to someone who understands the intricacies you face in your industry. We've found success in partnering not just with companies across the boardroom aisle but also with bigger entities. Electro Soft partnered with the Southeastern Pennsylvania Manufacturing Alliance (SEPMA), a multi-employer collaborative comprising regional manufacturers that work with education, workforce development, economic development, and community organizations to address the workforce and other competitiveness needs of the manufacturing industry.[70]

Through our relationship with them, we've developed a way of combating issues like developing and finding skilled labor. This partnership places us at the table to work through some of our most challenging issues as employers in the region. Together we cut through the cumbersome processes that exist in other institutions that keep us from moving forward in problem resolution. All voices at the table at the same time help move the process along quickly and efficiently. From our interaction with each other, an existing need emerged from our shared experiences. Through these relationships, solutions arise that we individually may not have seen before. As we continue to

---

69   UP-Rev.com, "13 Examples of Successful Co-Brand-
     ing Partnerships," accessed April 4, 2024, https://up-rev.
     com/13-examples-of-successful-co-branding-partnerships/#6.

70   Philadelphia Works, "About SEPMA," accessed April 4, 2024, https://philaworks.org/
     business-solutions/industry-partnerships/sepma/about-sepma/.

work together, I have found this partnership beneficial in helping both Electro Soft and the manufacturing industry.

A Survey of an Effective Manufacturing Partnership

In Pennsylvania, students must pass two Keystone Exams to graduate from high school. But what happens to the students who don't pass the exams and are ineligible to receive their diplomas? Enter Act 158, which provides alternative pathways to graduation.[71] One possibility is an evidence-based pathway, allowing students to obtain an industry-recognized credential to receive their diploma.[72] This pathway got my wheels turning. I could fulfill a dual need: create an alternative path for these students, and introduce them to the possibilities of working in manufacturing.

From that idea, I formed a small partnership, intending to identify students interested in electronics manufacturing. The vision is to give back to my immediate community by providing training for jobs, having an impact, and changing perspectives about manufacturing. This allows the students to enter the workforce with a steady full-time role with benefits, and they are able to build a life for themselves if college was not in their plans. The collective team vision is to create a continuous stream of skilled talent to restimulate the community's manufacturing workforce.

---

71   "Pennsylvania Graduation Requirements—Act 158," accessed April 4, 2024, https://www.wvwsd.org/site/handlers/filedownload.ashx?moduleinstanceid=560&dataid=4570&FileName=PENNSYLVANIA%20GRADUATION%20REQUIREMENTS%20for%20website%20158.pdf.

72   "Pennsylvania Graduation Requirements—Act 158."

But I knew I could not tackle this undertaking alone; I would need to take a collaborative approach. When creating partnerships, the goal is to align with people and entities to foster working relationships built on mutual trust. That is what our cross-functional team has developed. Within this partnership, we work on the mission as we provide one another with a sounding board and opportunity to leverage a brain trust. Recently, a team member shared with me that she had reached out to the state about her workforce development program several times, yet she couldn't get in touch with anyone. Using my connections, I was able to introduce them to her.

Presently, she meets monthly with them. My favorable referral of her work with our team gave her an added level of legitimacy. That's the beauty of partnership—the opportunities that arise. Good things happen when different people from various backgrounds convene to solve problems. As the concept of industry partnerships intends, our combined strengths create a means of accomplishing a bigger purpose. For example, my colleague brings her expertise in creating the training program to the table, while I bring my experience as an employer and business owner as well as my connections to other manufacturing companies. We transformed a budding idea into an established program that could potentially move forward and benefit the next crop of graduates.

We are presently piloting the program, but once it's solidified, we can create the playbook to share with other manufacturers so they can do the same. Once they master it and understand how the model works, we can share it with other in-demand careers throughout the Commonwealth of Pennsylvania. From there, we'll share with other states. Our cross-functional collaboration has the power to impact the careers of a generation of people who may not otherwise have many options.

Finding Strength in Numbers: Learning across the Aisle

When it was time for me to enhance the cybersecurity measures at Electro Soft, I had two options. I could connect with the scores of businesses that have reached out to me, none of which I know, and hope they would do the work properly. Or I could go into my network of professionals and reach out to someone whose ability I trust.

Because of my various relationships and partnerships, I was able to go with option two. I've been fortunate to find resources in networking spaces and organizations. My involvement with organizations like the Ernst & Young Entrepreneurs Access Network (EAN), the Ascend Cities program at the University of Washington, and the Advanced Management Entrepreneur Program (AMEP) at Northwestern University have all given me a community of diverse business owners, business experts, and university connections as well. Many of these programs have invested time and a budget to help get entrepreneurs to the next level, emphasizing entrepreneurs of color. They recognize the barriers we face. So, when all the members from those communities come together, plenty of opportunities exist for synergy and allyship. There is always power in like-minded connections.

When I have a question that arises in my daily operation, I'm able to reach out to the professionals I've connected with and get their insight. We also keep each other on top of trending information that could affect our businesses. If someone's company is dealing with a complex issue, we all weigh in, offering different solutions. From there we assist in formulating a plan of action. One of the groups continues to meet monthly via Zoom learning sessions, where we discuss cross-industry topics that others may be curious about.

In one of those Zoom sessions, our resident cybersecurity expert spoke about inexpensive low-hanging fruit areas for cybersecurity protection for small businesses. Typically, a business just starting out can't afford an annual five-figure investment in cybersecurity. However, it's a necessity that shouldn't be skimped on. A reported 60 percent of small businesses go out of business after a cyberattack.[73] What if the answer is as simple as one of the tactics outlined in our meeting, setting up two-step authentication? That simple solution can save a company thousands of dollars. That is just an example of how cross-collaborative relationships allow you to learn from other professionals who are not competing with you; they actually want you to win. The point is that partnerships and relationships can take many forms, but the purpose remains the same: working collaboratively for progression.

Strategic Partnerships

Although strategic partnerships are not new in the marketplace, they have become major in the business world by way of commercialized marketing. Strategic partnerships occur when two independent companies come together for a specific goal. It could be to expand their reach, get an edge, or further whatever growth they hope to gain. Also, it can simply be that the sole purpose is to make money from the same client base. Think of the Spotify and Uber strategic partnership—both companies are servicing the consumer in different ways, but they do it together.

As another example, I have two colleagues who were able to form a strategic partnership. One is in video production marketing, and the

73   Gary Smith, "+50 Cyber Attacks on Small Business Statistics," StationX.com, accessed April 6, 2024, https://www.stationx.net/cyber-attacks-on-small-businesses-statistics/#:~:text=A%20third%20of%20small%20business,and%20 subsequent%20small%20business%20failure.

other owns a marketing agency that creates written content and graphic design. Their agency doesn't do video content. As a team, they can go up against bigger agencies that have all services in-house. Together, they increase their visibility, which allows them to be seen and be viable among the other bidders. This enables them to win together.

Throughout manufacturing history, the United States has outsourced labor to Asia for decades, which was a major strategic power play ... until it wasn't. Asia's lower production cost due to cheaper labor and inexpensive material costs abroad put many stateside manufacturers at a disadvantage. US-based manufacturers couldn't compete. Although the trend is for companies to remove production from China, other countries are still acquiring larger accounts, more than US-based manufacturers.

As for the domestic side, smaller companies often lose jobs to larger businesses. Instead of losing those jobs, small businesses can create a joint partnership as a strategy to go after the same work, creating economies of scale, producing product at a lower price, and both coming out as winners. This merging of core competencies improves their collective chances of obtaining a particular contract. When it comes to strategic partnerships with other manufacturers, it's all about obtaining contracts.

As mentioned, partnerships come in many forms. There is some intersectionality, but the desired outcome makes them different. When working with schools, Electro Soft wants to be seen as a viable pipeline for graduates looking to enter the workforce post high school. Conversely, schools want to have a variety of options available to students who are planning futures outside college.

Taking a strategic move consists of seeking opportunities in new verticals in industries where you currently do not play. I'd love to see Electro Soft venture into emerging industries working on future-forward products that are currently changing the world. This is accomplished by securing a strategic acquisition. We did this in the dental industry because we didn't have a presence in the growing opportunities in dental electronics manufacturing. In the future, we will venture into other areas as well. It's always a good idea to be on the lookout for potential verticals that could expand your current offerings.

Reflection Points

• **Ditch the mindset of scarcity, and welcome a collaborative approach to growing your business!**

You'll be surprised how specific problems in manufacturing and other industries can be solved by collaboration.

• **Think of ways to position yourself to find all the opportunities you can.**

What business resource programs help businesses like yours? Commit to finding them, either locally or nationally. Doing this can enrich your business and network beyond measure. Also, join industry partnerships, and find out if your county or city has a workforce development or labor department. This will help you put together a partnership of similar industries. There are ways for you to get assistance right in your community. Find them.

- **Don't forget about your local school districts.**

If you want to reach students and get on their radar, especially if you are in manufacturing, schools can be your biggest assets. When they have career days, actually go and participate! Don't read about it later. Last, know legislation that can work in your favor similar to what my team did with the Pennsylvania Act 158. Find out if your state or county government has youth expos. We have the Careers of Tomorrow Annual Youth Expo, which highlights careers for our youth. Again, do your research!

- **Don't be so microfocused on the things you are doing. Take a moment to look up for a bit and discover new possibilities.**

Be able to "lean into the curves" of what's coming. Look beyond the opportunities outside your inbox and the ones that come to your doorstep. Leverage your networks and connections to align your company in lanes you may not have considered before. Be open.

CHAPTER NINE

Which Actions Will Help Us Create Generational Wealth?

Generational wealth isn't just about millions; it's about getting a leg up.

—Karla Trotman, CEO of Electro Soft

My introduction to generational wealth was an early one. When I was younger, I went to a Christian elementary school, and there were only two Black girls in my grade. I was one of them. Another one of our classmates, who was also my friend, was the child of a family business owner. I have memories of going to her family's home, and it was an amazing, beautiful place. They had an arcade in the basement, and she had a gorgeous room with a closet full of designer clothing, which is where I first learned about designer labels. I also remember going with her to her family business, where her family's last name sat proudly on the massive building, which was just as impressive as their home. I recall our spending the afternoon playing and running around in the lunchroom. Oh, and here's the best part—she spent some months away from school one year because her family went to Japan to grow their business.

At the time, I didn't know the magnitude of what I was experiencing. All I knew was that they had an impressive life. I learned later that her grandfather and father had started the business. When we met as children, her father was the president of the company. Later in life she and her brothers grew the company by leveraging private equity investment and later sold it. And now, they're doing work on boards and pursuing other professional endeavors. My biggest observation was that the family business afforded them opportunities. That was my first example of the possibilities generational wealth could achieve.

Coincidentally, the other Black girl in my class was the child of an entrepreneurial family as well. Her father owned an ambulatory service and a limo company. For my tenth birthday, she had her dad pick us up in a limo and take us to the roller-skating rink and to the mall afterward to celebrate. It was cool, because I got to see a Black entrepreneur living successfully while my father had just started Electro Soft. Again, none of this impacted me until years later. It did, however, show me the benefits of having independently sourced income.

When this same friend had her birthday, her uncle surprised her by having Wanya Morris, of the multiplatinum Grammy award–winning R&B group Boyz II Men, sing "Happy Birthday" to her in her father's living room. At the time, Boyz II Men was huge, so we sat in awe as he performed. As if that wasn't big enough, her parties became even more impressive. I remember years later as teenagers, for another one of her birthday parties, we went to her father's newly constructed home.

Keep in mind that back then, global positioning systems (GPS) didn't exist. Me and my best friend Tammy read directions from the invitation and ultimately thought we had gotten lost. Struggling and frustrated, I saw a museum up the road ahead and suggested to her that we go there and ask for help. As we got closer, we noticed a banner across the pillars wishing my friend a happy birthday. We had arrived at the new mansion her father had built for his family.

The party was amazing! She had African stilt walkers, and there was a dance floor in the basement. It was legendary—truly a teenager's dream party. Unknowingly, these experiences planted a belief in my subconscious mind that starting a business was the pathway to financial security.

As I continued to grow and live more, I saw that the ultimate value creation lies in the small business; it is a catalyst for obtaining generational wealth. The US educational system sensationalizes going to college to get a good-paying job and ultimately vying for a C-suite position, but what I had experienced in my own life was a different approach to success.

Although the path to obtaining generational wealth through a successful small business is challenging, it can be done. By understanding the foundational elements of establishing generational wealth, why it's vital to a family structure, and how to maintain it, we can ensure our families are active players in accumulating wealth.

Handling Critical Family Business

People tend to place a high dollar value on the phrase *generational wealth*. However, the "wealth" aspect differs based on the circumstances. The wealth could be an eight-figure business that transitions from one generation to the next, or it can be $10,000 and a food truck. Generational wealth occurs on many different levels, just as small businesses occur in different iterations. Wealth is wealth and should be handled accordingly to preserve its utility. Whatever you own, you must prioritize how it will live on beyond you. This is done by following some crucial steps.

Once Black-owned businesses surpass the societal barriers of securing funding to grow and scale, one of the essential ways to maintain generational wealth is to strategize. This is accomplished by solidifying essential documents necessary for the transference of wealth. Regardless of the amount of wealth, estate planning, creating a will, and end-of-life activity documents are critical to have in place. These measures protect whatever legacy families are leaving behind for future generations. Without the formation of these documents, any bank accounts or assets could be held in probate and the wealth transfers would be lost. Sadly, Black families are five times less likely than white families to receive a sizable inheritance, if any.[74]

This statistic can be improved by families handling their business. And I don't mean creating a will on a legal pad and filing it away in a cabinet or drawer. Creating a will properly means going through the channels and hiring a lawyer. This is important because a will is a living document that requires frequent edits as life and circumstances change. Adding any changes is valuable to keeping the document viable. It's also important to have the will created at the appropriate time of the will holder's life.

Although it varies from state to state and it's wise to seek legal counsel regarding the specifics of a given situation, if someone dies

---

74   "Black Wealth Transfer and Confronting the Racial Wealth Gap," Bloomberg. com, accessed April 7, 2024, https://www.bloomberg.com/company/stories/ black-wealth-transfer-and-confronting-the-racial-wealth-gap/.

without a will, it's deemed as dying intestate.[75] If at the time of death there is no will and there is no instruction on who obtains what assets, then the state gets involved. The assets enter the probate process, and attempts will be made to find the appropriate heir.[76]

Again, depending on the state, the probate process can be timely. It can last anywhere from two weeks to two years, causing funds to be tied up or lost.[77] That's why it's important for adults as young as eighteen years old to have a will. These measures ensure, at the very least, that your family members won't have to have a GoFundMe campaign to simply cover the costs of putting you into the ground. There are so many more effective solutions. Even having a small insurance policy of $25,000 can take the burden off many family members upon your demise. The younger you are, the cheaper the policy.

For older family members, it's important to form a will before they transition. If this is not done, conflict among the remaining family members over the possession of homes and other assets could result. More than likely, because there isn't a will in place, legal professionals will get involved. The lawyer fees and other court assessments can dwindle the full value of what families could have passed to the next generation. Having the proper paperwork created and filed with an attorney could preempt this reduction.

Having these crucial documents in order is more important now than ever before. As a society, we're about to lose a lot of members of

75   Brette Sember, JD, "Intestate Succession: What Happens When You Die without a Will," LegalZoom, accessed April 29, 2024, https://www.legalzoom.com/articles/intestate-succession-what-happens-when-you-die-without-a-will.

76   Sember, "Intestate Succession: What Happens When You Die without a Will."

77   Ashley Kilroy, "How Long Does Probate Take?" accessed April 8, 2024, https://smartasset.com/estate-planning/how-long-does-probate-take.

DARK, DIRTY, DANGEROUS

the baby boomer generation, and there will be a huge wealth transfer.[78] Their transitioning means that many Gen Xers and millennials will be forced to go through the probate process because their families have not taken the proper steps. My dad did not want us to become one of those instances, so he planned accordingly.

As adults, my dad called my brothers and me to the company conference room and gave us a copy of his will to read through. The goal was for us to understand what his wishes were and to ask questions if we had any. I was one of the executors of his estate, and as we read through the will, I didn't understand one of the clauses and asked if I was interpreting it correctly. Since we were all present, I was able to get clarity at that moment and preemptively protect the will from what I felt could cause a future lawsuit. I mentioned that if I didn't understand the clause, others could misinterpret it as well. My dad agreed, so he made changes with his lawyer and had it codified in the will.

That's the beauty of handling business before someone transitions—it provides the opportunity to clear up any misunderstandings or confusion. In that meeting, we were all able to collectively ask questions and get on the same page. We met for only one hour, and it saved us from future arguments and a potential legal battle. When that unfortunate time comes and our dad is no longer with us, we all have the plan of action, because we took the time to get on the same page.

---

78   Jack Kelly, "The Great Wealth Transfer from Baby Boomers to Millennials Will Impact the Job Market and Economy," *Forbes*, August 9, 2023, https://www.forbes.com/sites/jackkelly/2023/08/09/the-great-wealth-transfer-from-baby-boomers-to-millennials-will-impact-the-job-market-and-economy/?sh=53885c313e4a.

Stop Playing Small, Level Up

When it comes to securing your family's future, the power play is finding ways to transfer wealth while you are still living. Typically, these strategies are hidden in plain sight. There are different levels of wealth accumulation, and we don't readily know of these other possibilities. The information isn't always shared. That's why I am including it in this book. This topic is so important to me; I want as many people as possible to know their options.

As we start accumulating wealth as business owners, there is a chance the bank we're using to service our businesses today will not be able to service our businesses tomorrow. We outgrow their services and offerings. However, many of us are as committed to our banks as we are to our churches, but you need to change your mindset. Your bank should be working for you. You give them the ability to lend out your money. In return, they should be offering products and services commensurate with your level of assets. A strong banking relationship can be a game changer as you grow your business and ultimately your net worth. You want a bank that understands your business needs and goals and can offer you advice and services to meet both.

Level up the ways that you finance your company. After you have invested your own funds, completed a round of friends-and-family fundraising, and gone to a bank and received debt capital, it may be time to consider equity capital. During that time, you are giving ownership interest to another party in exchange for equity in your business. Often that means they now have a say in the way you run the business as an owner. This can be good or bad depending on a number of factors, such as whether you want total control over your company, have the experience to take it to the next level, or have access to additional markets. There are many things to consider.

You must ask yourself, "Do I want to be the 100 percent owner of a $2 million revenue-generating company or a 50 percent owner of a $50 million revenue-generating company?" These partnerships can contribute to exponential growth. I want to drive this point home and be clear. Generational wealth doesn't just happen. With planning, strategy implementation, and strong connections, wealth accumulation is possible.

I was introduced to wealth accumulation at a young age. I walked into my dad's office one day, and he showed me how a stock he'd purchased at one price increased in value by simply sitting in his account. At that moment, I was obsessed with learning how to invest money in the stock market. My parents created custodial brokerage accounts for me and my brothers, then bought us stock that grew over time, which we took over when we turned eighteen. Those starter accounts were small investments, but they grew over time. That is the beauty of compounding. When we gained control, we had been given a head start. We were able to either sell the stock or allow it to continue to grow. The gift was more than stock; it was the gift of options.

Opening and funding custodial brokerage accounts is another method of wealth transfer. I still have some of those initial shares today, and other times I've sold shares to help me get through some tough times in life. That is one of the many gifts my parents gave me that helped me level up. I then in turn did the same for my sons by opening their custodial accounts. They weren't as excited as I was when I got mine, but at least they will know the power of compounding through these accounts.

In business, leveling up requires that you get out of the patterns you're used to and see your company's full potential from a different perspective. When I took over the company, my dad told me that

Electro Soft was a great lifestyle business. It affords the opportunity to do so many things! You can travel, pay off your home mortgage, send your kids to school, and just live a good life in general. He told me to enjoy the perks and that I didn't have to worry about growing the company. Cool! That worked for me.

But then I went to the invitation-only Strategic Growth Forum, Ernst & Young's annual entrepreneur conference. While I was there, I met other entrepreneurs doing exactly what I did, but they were performing at a higher level than me. I was blown away! Until then, I didn't realize the kind of money that could be made in electronics manufacturing! It's because my perception of the business had been what my dad mentioned—it was a lifestyle business. We were tinkering away, doing projects for people in our little bubble. It was comfortable.

That is why I mention the importance of leveling up your environment. It causes your reality to shift, and you can explore the possibilities. I learned from this conference that the work we do is in high demand. So, when I met people who were sitting at a $60 million valuation, it made me take a step back and ask myself, "Why am I playing it so small?" The adage is true: if you can see it, you can be it. Let me tell you, until that conference, I'd never seen it … or the pathway to it!

Now that I knew better, I could do better. When I got back home and started unpacking, it hit me: *we need to hit $100 million.* Shortly thereafter, I connected with someone I met at the conference. As we closed the conversation, he said to me, "We'll finish this conversation after you make your first $100 million." This random reference marked the second time the number had come up in my consciousness. Then in a third random conversation, that number came up again!

My eyes were now open. I realized that if we were to achieve this goal, I needed to make some major changes. I went back to the drawing board and dismantled our existing business structure. I created an advisory board, worked with my business coach on a new strategy, and changed my entire attitude toward how this business was going to break out of being a lifestyle brand and focus on growth and scale. Each decision I made thereafter was structured around that $100 million goal post. The bottom line is, new information requires a new plan to get to new levels.

To get your business to the next level and ready for a seamless transition to future generations, you must invest in yourself. When I first started considering taking over the company, my father told me there was no need to finish my MBA, that he'd teach me all I needed to know. What I discovered was that he could teach me, but it would be like being in an echo chamber. I knew that in order for me to take this business from entrepreneurial to professional, it was going to require a deeper level of business understanding that could only be attained at a university.

So, I went back to school, but I chose to get an executive MBA as opposed to a traditional MBA. It was the right move for me because I couldn't see myself going to school with twenty-somethings with little work experience. At that time in my career, I had expertise, and I wanted to leverage that experiential learning and deconstruct my experiences with other professionals. I'm glad I did. Going back to school caused my inner intellectual to awaken.

Drexel's executive MBA program starts with each candidate working with an executive coach. Executive coaching is one of the greatest known unknowns in business. In theory, I've always known of executive coaches, but I truly never knew what they did. They are secret strategists who help you achieve stronger performance levels in business. Some of today's most well-respected professionals use coaches but never let on that they have them.

Many business professionals require their executive coaches to sign nondisclosure agreements because a stigma exists about not being self-made in one's business success. Going back to school completely erased that stigma for me. I now saw the power in coaching. And not only did I learn how to become a better thinker but the investment in self gave me the confidence to accomplish the task of growing my family business.

Consider this. Where do we get examples of leadership otherwise? Other than the fictitious depictions of toxic bosses in movies and television? People don't typically go to school to learn how to be good managers, supervisors, or trainers. Also, companies typically don't invest in leadership development, because their focus is mainly on the soft skills required for working in higher-level management. That's why going to school and learning leadership and effective business practices to run a business are so important.

It was here that I was first introduced to the possibility of doing mergers and acquisitions. Prior to graduate school I thought they only happened on a grander scale. During this time I decided that buying another company that may not have a succession plan would be a viable option for Electro Soft. With my newfound knowledge and confidence, we were able to buy the company without a deal team. It ended up being one of the most cost-effective moves we have made to increase revenue for the company during that time. That's the beauty of my executive MBA. I could leave class and implement the strategies right away!

After graduating, I realized I needed additional help and made another investment in hiring my own executive coach. She was well known in my manufacturing entrepreneur circle, as they all had used her previously. Hey, there is no shame in getting help with direction. Those entrepreneurs were helpful in showing me that this particular coach would be a wonderful support in helping me take a first-generation company to the second generation. Ensuring Electro Soft's continued growth was a skill set I had not yet developed. And I was not embarrassed to get help. It has never been beneath me to ask for help.

Also, don't forget to invest in your children. Investing in them is an extension of investing in yourself. That's the beauty of building generational wealth through a family business. It's a cycle. I benefited from the hard work of my parents' commitment to build Electro Soft. Now I'm preparing my kids for the future, helping them to develop their vision of ownership. If you are a business owner with children, I urge you to start planting seeds to gauge their interest in the business and its operations. Allow them to understand that to be owners, they don't have to work in the business, but they need to understand the business and finances. This understanding is not going to be innate; it must be taught and trained.

Now that my sons are getting older, our investment professional is training them on proper financial literacy and sharing with them the status of their accounts. Educating them about money will hopefully deter a "new money" mentality when they become business owners. Proper education helps them know that they have the distinct privilege and honor of taking the reins of a company, an investment tool, to grow it even further. When they are out of school for the summer, I have them come to board meetings so they can learn how an advisory board works. Even if they are bored, I've told them it doesn't matter. The point is that they are there, sitting and listening, and they will be required to ask questions. Outside that, my sons have the flexibility to be involved in industry-adjacent summer activities like engineering camps so they can explore their interests. Again, it's all about planting the seeds.

Get Comfortable with Delaying Gratification

Often what gets overshadowed in the glory of entrepreneurship are the inherent sacrifices that come with taking the path less traveled— business ownership. When starting out with my new family, we lived below our means. That meant making decisions with the best financial outcome in mind. For instance, during the real estate bubble, we opted for two smaller townhomes as opposed to one single-family home. Also, we leaned on family members for day care, and were diligent savers. We even kept our first little townhome as a rental property in an effort to build up our balance sheet.

I mentioned earlier that my friends were able to buy dream homes and live fabulous lives; well, we were not able to do that then. It was during that time that I started my online business, using savings and a credit card (a veritable B-school no-no.) But when the bubble burst, we were in a solid position, as none of our properties were underwater and we weren't living paycheck to paycheck. And when the time came to purchase my family business, our hard work and dedication paid off.

My balance sheet was solid, my credit was excellent, and I had accumulated a solid business acumen in online marketing, SEO, website development, supplier negotiation, and more. I used that time of delay to ready myself for the next big step. This was also how we were able to afford our forever home before I took over Electro Soft. We ignored the Joneses so that we could invest and save for our future.

A principle I live by is to be like the Rockefellers, not the Vanderbilts. The Vanderbilts gave cash to the next generation, who spent it.

The Rockefellers invested their wealth in people and their businesses. That created a legacy in which future generations can live off the interest of that wealth. By leaning into frugality and investment principles, I ended up gaining and making my money stretch to double the return on my investment. If I'm honest, I don't think there's anything I have bought that has made me feel great in the long term. But saving money or having money available for myself and my family in the future makes me feel great. Hopefully, when I leave this Earth, I'll be leaving things to honor what my parents have built—for future generations to have a better life.

Bonus: Get an All-Star Advisory Board

In my opinion, advisory boards are crucial to sustaining and elevating your business. An advisory board has no fiduciary responsibility, but the input of its members is worth its weight in platinum based on the advice they provide. I mentioned Electro Soft's board earlier but want to share details on how it works. In our meetings, we go over any historical items discussed in prior meetings that I've acted on, and I share how things landed. Then the Electro Soft fractional chief financial officer (CFO), who is an ex officio member of the board, presents on the company's previous-quarter financial performance and how we are tracking for the year. We end with a review of the strategic plan and tackle any issues that may keep us from hitting the mark.

Truthfully, we spend a lot of time on the financial side of the business because my board is heavily invested in understanding how we spend money and where we make our money. Their expertise is invaluable. That is the benefit of having a board. We are seven mighty minds of diverse backgrounds and experiences, debating and molding the future of Electro Soft. From forceful to suggestive, it's all in that one room. This is why having a cross-functional advisory board is one of the most valuable tools you can have as a business owner. They help you find blind spots you wouldn't readily see, and they help you zip right around those obtuse learning curves for a bigger impact.

Reflection Points

• **Generational wealth does not have to be millions or even thousands of dollars. Don't diminish the work of one generation by failing to create the paperwork to preserve it.**

Start with getting a simple will made for each adult member of the family, and then go over it to ensure there is no confusion about the terms. Your future generations will thank you.

• **Know the different levels of financing that can level up your company and organizations to various types of financial gain.**

There are many ways to expand your businesses; you just have to be aware of them and take advantage. The biggest flex is building your wealth while you are still alive. Use it!

• **Consider hiring a coach.**

There is no shame in getting help in areas where you could use development. Working with a coach can enrich the quality of input you share with your company.

• **Build a strong board of advisors.**

Recently, a colleague who works with high-net-worth business owners mentioned that she could count on one hand the number of companies she knows that have an advisory board. I highly suggest you create a strong board of around five advisors if you are truly seeking to grow and/or succeed your company. Their advice is invaluable as it pertains to increasing the value of your business and ultimately creating generational wealth for your family.

CHAPTER TEN

How Can We Prepare for the Future of Electronics Manufacturing?

My hard work is finally catching up with perfect timing.

—Future

Preparing for the future of manufacturing is a massive undertaking. Before we discuss how to prepare for the future, let's take a look back at the past, particularly the Industrial Revolution and its different phases. It took about eighty years for the switch from steam technology to the Second Industrial Revolution, which featured steel, electricity, mechanical engineering, and advances in communication and transportation.[79] Then it took seventy-four years for the third

---

79   Centre of Excellence, "Unveiling the Industrial Revolution: Facts, Inventions, and Impact," Centre of Excellence, accessed April 14, 2024, https://www.centreofexcellence.com/industrial-revolution-timeline/.

revolution to take place.[80] Now, 264 years later, we are in the Fourth Industrial Revolution. Technology is moving at a speed that inventors and scientists of years past could not even imagine! This revolution is marked by the convergence of digitization, artificial intelligence (AI), and the mass of information on the internet.

Essentially, in this revolution, we are witnessing the merger of the physical and digital world. Again, how do you plan for a future with so many unknowns? What comes to mind is Moore's law. Formed in 1965, Gordon Moore's law states that the number of transistors on a microchip doubles about every two years with a minimal cost increase.[81] This movement predicates that computing processing capabilities double every two years, which they have since 1970.[82] Technology is changing so quickly, which produces subsequent societal progression to occur faster. Attempting to guess the future of technology is like trying to capture lightning in a bottle and sell it on Amazon.

Every day we're faced with innovation that even in its beginning stages is changing the way we think and how our workforce works. With the introduction of technological tools like AI into the mainstream, the way workers perform their roles is changing. These advances allow workers to increase utility and work more efficiently. And there are more of them on the way. According to the World Economic Forum report *The Future of Jobs from 2016*, 65 percent of children in primary schools today will be working in jobs that don't

---

80   Centre of Excellence. "Unveiling the Industrial Revolution: Facts, Inventions, and Impact."

81   Carla Tardi, "What Is Moore's Law and Is It Still True?" Investopedia.com, accessed April 10, 2024, https://www.investopedia.com/terms/m/mooreslaw. asp#:~:text=Moore's%20Law%20states%20that%20the%20number%20of%20 transistors%20on%20a,became%20known%20as%20Moore's%20Law.

82   Tardi, "What Is Moore's Law and Is It Still True?"

exist yet.[83] That statistic was projected eight years ago—imagine how nearly impossible it is to envision this ever-evolving future.

Because of this speed, it's hard to even nail down where Electro Soft or manufacturing will be in five years, let alone ten years. But this doesn't mean I have not outlined a vision for my company's future. I hope that Electro Soft is one of multiple companies in a portfolio of businesses within the manufacturing sector. And this is not necessarily in vertical markets alone but also in complimentary markets to support innovation in several ways. This projected future growth is aligned with our mission to help other companies innovate with our technical ability and savvy. It's an ideal partnership presently and foreseeably for the future. Visionary companies are going to need partners that can perform the applied aspect of their innovation. There is a need, and we have the solution for the demand. That's where I see Electro Soft thriving—in the future in the industrial electronics manufacturing marketplace.

In terms of the electronics manufacturing industry, I think there will be a shift in priorities in this technological landscape. This shift will cause companies to focus on production autonomy in a way they've never experienced before. From in-house 3D printing and the introduction of AI efficiencies and beyond, the shrinking supply chain is causing the game to change. Then I sense there will be more focus on an area that has been taken for granted for far too long, the health and well-being of the global marketplace top commodity—its people. While the trend is not just specific to manufacturing, businesses will need to weigh the social ramifications of a workforce facing social anomalies. Lastly, I imagine increased attention being paid to

---

83   Ernst & Young, "How to Prepare Our Children for Jobs That Don't Exist Yet," accessed April 10, 2024, https://www.ey.com/es_es/workforce/your-child_s-job-probably-doesnt-exist-yet.

cybersecurity and cyberwelfare, which will play a major role in the future of electronics manufacturing.

Becoming Agile: Focusing on the Individual

In 2020, our nation's definition of how we work changed and created a dichotomic shift that has shaped our new normal. Due to the pandemic, jobs moved from working in person to working from a home office, which was an unprecedented change. Between 2019 and 2021, the number of people primarily working from home tripled from 5.7 percent (roughly 9 million people) to 17.9 percent (27.6 million people), according to the 2021 American Community Survey (ACS).[84]

This transition could not have come at a more unique time, because we were already a society experiencing certain levels of isolation due to the internet boom in tandem with social media use. With the average American spending nearly five hours a day on their phone and two-and-a-half of those hours on social media, we are becoming less tactile socially and relegated to socializing through screens.[85,86]

---

84   United States Census, "The Number of People Primarily Working from Home Tripled Between 2019 and 2021," accessed April 14, 2024, https://www.census.gov/ newsroom/press-releases/2022/people-working-from-home.html.

85   Emily Volz, "Screen Time Addiction? The Average American Spends 4.5 Hours per Day on Phone," NBC 10 News, accessed April 14, 2024, https://turnto10.com/i-team/ consumer-advocate/screen-time-addiction-average-american-spends-four-hours- per-day-phone-younger-generation-reduce-laptops-notifications-january-22-2024.

86   Josh Howarth, "Worldwide Daily Social Media Usage (New 2024 Data)," Explod- ingTopics.com, accessed April 14, 2024, https://explodingtopics.com/blog/ social-media-usage.

Social separation causes people to feel isolated and alone, which in turn affects how people interact and show up to work. Prolonged social media usage is linked to depression, social anxiety, and other mental illnesses that affect adults. More importantly, these afflictions are widespread among adolescents, who are the future of our workforce.[87] The workforce of the future will need to have a higher emotional quotient (EQ) when potentially dealing with someone diagnosed in one of these areas. It would benefit anyone in a forward-facing role to be well versed in how to interact with these mentally diverse individuals.

Additionally, leaders will need to learn how to connect with employees on an emotional level and read body language from the chest up through Zoom. Videoconferencing has replaced the telephone and has become the more connective communication. Software is even being developed by lead videoconferencing software Zoom that will detect human emotion in meetings, intending to create stronger connection.[88]

These developments will help leaders connect with their team remotely, but the reality is that we are sentient beings that crave in-person community. On worksites, a newly required onus will be put on electronic manufacturing companies to build an environment of trust and connection to maintain a sense of community in their work culture. To do this, it's more important than ever that companies be agile.

---

87 Kathy Katella, "How Social Media Affects Your Teen's Mental Health: A Parent's Guide," Yale Medicine, accessed April 14, 2024, https://www.yalemedicine.org/news/social-media-teen-mental-health-a-parents-guide#:~:text=According%20to%20a%20research%20study%20of%20American,to%20a%20higher%20relative%20concern%20of%20harm.

88 Nadeem Sarwar, "Zoom Wants to Track Your Emotions, Here's What You Should Know," ScreenRant, accessed May 28, 2024, https://screenrant.com/zoom-emotion-tracking-ai-invasive-appeal/.

Business agility is defined as a progressive, people-centric approach to all aspects of business, ensuring its longevity in the modern world.[89] This occurs by focusing on individuals, not being tone-deaf, identifying and correlating societal factors, and relating them to their work environments. People are not OK, and these factors affect their performance and overall health. This is a huge shift for electronics manufacturers to prioritize mental wellness. Back in the day, it was the same routine daily. Go to work, punch a clock, do the work, and leave. Little to no attention was paid to workers' well-being. But now, workers want to like where they are going as well as the work they are doing there.

The companies that form that care and consideration around their people will thrive. Now, this doesn't necessarily mean holding a quarterly T-shirt day or team spirit day, but it does mean offering insurance benefits or an EAP to help workers navigate mental health challenges. If it's not a full policy, it should at least cover a portion so workers don't debate getting the help they need versus paying the bills. At Electro Soft we are not obligated to offer insurance, but we do. Additionally, we offer 60 percent off costs, not just for the employee but for their entire family. It's just the right thing to do; it's not always about the gross margin.

Although many electronics manufacturing companies can't contribute to the remote workforce boom, they can create their version of it by allowing flexible work hours. This allows parents to put their children on the bus in the morning and to be home when they get off the bus. It's all about evolving past simple empathy and ingenuity to take care of your people. This is also important because the future workforce has options.

---

89 Agile Business Consortium, "Business Agility," https://www.agilebusiness.org/business-agility.html.

In previous chapters, we've gone deeply into the demographics of the future of the manufacturing workforce, which will consist of immigrants, diverse individuals, younger workers, and women. This future workforce will have different standards. Specifically, they have an awareness that other generations that preceded them didn't. We've seen how this next generation is rethinking higher education via colleges and universities. They realize there are many majors and areas of study that are going to be obsolete based on the inability to find jobs to justify the cost of tuition. They are seeing more practical ways to earn a living through the trades, freelancing, and leveraging tools. To keep them engaged, we must treat them right.

DEI Is a Tool—It Isn't Political

During the publishing of this book, the DEI initiative has been harshly scrutinized. It's foreseeable that companies will not be required to pay attention to it in the future. Although it won't be required, making it a priority is advisable. Instead of viewing it as a political vice to be removed, it should be looked upon as a tool to leverage business. I would advise that companies take everything they've heard in the last few years in the media, in the political world, and around the watercooler and realize that DEI is a tool to leverage better business. Diversity not only benefits the environment but can drive profits. Diverse companies experience a 2.5 percent profit increase per employee, and diverse teams are 35 percent more productive.[90] These

---

90   Laura Wood, "Diversity and Inclusion (D&I) Global Market Report 2022: Diverse Companies Earn 2.5 Times Higher Cash Flow per Employee and Inclusive Teams Are More Productive by Over 35%," Global Newswire.com, accessed April 14, 2024, https://www.globenewswire.com/news-release/2022/08/09/2494604/0/en/Diversity-and-Inclusion-D-I-Global-Market-Report-2022-Diverse-Companies-Earn-2-5-Times-Higher-Cash-Flow-Per-Employee-and-Inclusive-Teams-Are-More-Productive-by-Over-35.html.

stats show the benefits of DEI and why pursuing it in the future will be beneficial in all work environments.

My Future as President

In the future, I don't see myself as the President of Electro Soft. Although this is a family business, I think there'll be a point when it would make sense for someone else to take it to the next level. This person doesn't have to be a member of the family. I see my future working with other diverse companies, helping them work through the issues of generational succession planning. I want to give them a pathway using empathy through the transition. I feel called to that because it is one of the fastest ways to help bridge the wealth gap.

I think my story isn't so different from that of a lot of other family businesses, but I realize you don't know what you don't know. We just need to have more conversations about wealth transfer. Again, one more dollar will not increase my marginal utility. However, if on my deathbed I can say that I was able to make an impact in the transference of wealth from generation to generation, I'll be really happy. I'm grateful to have used Electro Soft as a tool to teach others how to establish generational wealth and to inspire the power of legacy. It's created a community of people who have been supportive and proud to work for our family business.

Of all the amazing things I've learned, I'm not just going to take them to the grave. I'm going to share them and help as many people as I can. In the near future, once I'm done filling in all the foundational holes and getting the company to a good place, I hope it becomes a great example of the American dream for people of color. There are many stories of other family-owned Black businesses that have been plagued with toxicity. I want Electro Soft's story to be the opposite.

I want it to be a good story. An empowering one. I want families to take what we've learned and shared and create generational wealth for themselves. My future looks like educating my community by arming them with the tools they need to succeed. That's the goal.

Reflection Points

• Taking care of the future workforce means treating them as if they are more than just an employee number. Nurturing employees will keep them happy, causing them to produce more. Doing this means a dedicated commitment to staying on top of societal changes and morphing company culture to be as inclusive as possible.

Being flexible is the answer to adapting to the inevitable change of the future. There is no possible way to know what's ahead, but the control companies and workers have is their readiness for the change. The key is to notice societal changes and make parallels in the work environment with people-first directives. The future belongs to agile businesses.

• In whatever capacity you are working presently, ask yourself if it is aligned with the vision you have for your future. Use your company or present role as a tool to get you where your career path is calling you. Every part of your journey can inspire others and will set a precedent to position you where you are needed in the future.

Be honest with yourself. I encourage you to ask yourself the question that Sam Johnson, Ernst & Young VP of accounts, asked me during their Strategic Growth Forum in November 2023: "Are you the best person to run your company?" To answer this, it's necessary to have a clear vision of where you want your company to go. Elevation may require someone with a different skill set. Have the ability to recognize this and employ the proper executive.

CONCLUSION

Did you hear about the rose that grew from a crack in the concrete? Proving nature's laws wrong, it learned to walk without having feet. Funny it seems, but by keeping its dreams, it learned to breathe fresh air. Long live the rose that grew from concrete when no one else even cared.

—Tupac Shakur

During the writing of this book, many changes took place in the nation. From an unstable economy to the emergence of wars causing a change in the political climate, a lot was going on. Then there were the internal changes at Electro Soft—from onboarding new staff to gaining new resources to enhance their experience as a part of our team. But that is the reality of business; it is filled with ups and downs. These changes, both internally and externally, impacted the content of this book.

This project began with my intention to help those desiring a career in manufacturing. As I began to write, it morphed into more. It became an ode to my parents' dedication to create a solid financial future for their family. That in turn inspired me to pay homage to other pioneering Black families. Those families against all odds fought for financial independence with their businesses.

I realized in telling their stories and mine that I have a newfound admiration for the strength of those who accomplish the seemingly impossible. That is the underlying theme of this book—the bravery and determination it takes to accomplish greatness regardless of the obstacles.

Aptly, the final section of this book appropriately opened with a quote from the prolific philosopher of his time, hip-hop legend Tupac Shakur. The quote depicts the story of a rose that has emerged from seemingly impossible circumstances, growing from concrete. It is a metaphor for the beautifully challenging lives of Black Americans. I contend that we are that rose. Given our ancestors' introduction to this country decades ago, we really were not supposed to make it. Yet here we are. Our roses continuously bloom. Through the roughest terrain, we make it. We make the impossible possible when we keep going.

In Chapter 10, we looked to the future. My prediction is that we will continue to persevere and stop merely surviving but will begin to thrive. The future looks like more opportunities, finding effective ways to finance our businesses, and securing independence by forming generational wealth. This book, with Electro Soft as its case study, serves as a guide to establishing and protecting a family business and seeing it through to succession. What's unique is that each generation has a role to play. My parents laid the foundation, and I continued the legacy by adding my education, advisory council, and some tools that I have picked up along the way in order to keep it growing.

One of the biggest assets to success is getting out into your community and making connections. There is power in expanding your network and finding mutually beneficial relationships. The ideal goal is to find like-minded strategic partners, either through organizations or fellow companies. We can make it to our destinations on our own, but it's so much better and easier with help. There is power in expanding your reach outside your comfort zone to find the people and opportunities to make progress and growth easier.

Keep this in mind: while on your path, be sure to realize the role you play in your company and your perception in the marketplace. As a leader, the biggest proof of the stability of your business is your team. Satisfied employees are the benchmark of a healthy and productive company. Your day-to-day responsibilities as the CEO or president of your company showcase your ability to lead. I urge you to let your employees know that they work with you and not just for you.

Cultivating a team mentality builds a sense of community. It's better to have a leader who works alongside their team instead of barking commands from an elevated glass-paned office. If you are a leader of color like me, you will face many odds, but with determination, expertise, and collectivism, you can solidify yourself in a position to succeed. The playing field has never been even, but we have the power to inspire and elevate our existing and future employees with effective leadership methods. We are the example.

As it relates to members of the future workforce, we've identified that they are different from any we've encountered before. Where past generations may have obstructed diversity, the younger new generations thrive in it. These young workers will demand better working conditions and an environment conducive to their development. By fostering a work environment with empathy and respect, companies stand to attract young, driven talent. It's all about meeting their needs and understanding the trends that predicate their differences.

Once you have a solid team of employees, always realize that at the beginning and end of the day, it is about the clients. You are not the only player in town who can do what you do. Today's consumer has so many options. Stand out by providing quality work and including your personal touch as often as you can. Don't always work behind the screen or over the phone. Grab some treats and make visits to your clients whenever possible. That lets them know they're dealing with a person and not a facade behind a device.

Black women and women of color working in barrier industries, know this: although it is true that your experience is different from that of your male counterparts, you have the freedom to show up as your whole authentic self. We are not working in the old raggedy industries of decades past. We are here and are reshaping what CEOs and presidents look like in these industries. Being "the first" or one of a few is an honor. You are in a lane that didn't exist as frequently before. Proudly show up in the room, and add your expertise and innovation.

As we close, I'm excited to know it's a brand-new day for electronics manufacturing. I've come a long way from the little girl cutting wire when Electro Soft first began. The adjectives used in the title of this book—*dark*, *dirty*, and *dangerous*—mirror the preconceived notions I had for manufacturing in the 1980s when my parents founded Electro Soft. The three words reflect how others may view the industry currently. However, it's my hope that by having shared my story and exploring the possibilities of this multifaceted industry, it will be seen in a new light. I truly believe that with added awareness and a focus on innovation, manufacturing will finally be seen in its new vibrant hue.

Contact

Would you like to continue the conversation further?

Contact me or learn about the latest in manufacturing and trending information on business, generational wealth, and more by scanning the QR codes below!

KarlaTrotman.com/Contact

ElectroSoftInc.com

About the Author

Karla Trotman, the CEO and president of Electro Soft, Inc., is a native of Montgomery County, Pennsylvania. From a young age, Karla witnessed her parents' dedication and determination in building Electro Soft from the ground up. Despite her initial reluctance to follow in their footsteps, Karla's unique journey ultimately led her back to the family business.

Before successfully acquiring Electro Soft, Karla gained invaluable experience working in various roles at notable companies such as Honeywell, Gap, and IKEA, where she honed her skills in supply chain logistics, purchasing, and e-commerce. Her entrepreneurial spirit also led her to establish an online boutique that garnered a celebrity and international clientele, further showcasing her business acumen and drive for success.

Karla's professional achievements are a testament to her dedication and passion for excellence. Her journey to becoming the CEO of Electro Soft was not without its challenges, as she navigated the complex process of succession planning and ownership transition. Through perseverance, strategic decision-making, and the support of her family and trusted advisors, Karla successfully acquired the company, ensuring that her parents' legacy would continue to thrive under her leadership.

In addition to her role at Electro Soft, Karla is an active member of her community, sitting on several boards and lending her expertise to various organizations. She is a strong advocate for diversity and inclusion in the workplace, and she is committed to fostering a company culture that values authenticity, innovation, and collaboration.

Karla's experience as a second-generation business owner has given her a unique perspective on the challenges and rewards of running a family business. Through this book, she aims to share her insights and strategies for success, offering guidance and inspiration to aspiring entrepreneurs and business leaders.

When she's not leading Electro Soft to new heights, Karla cherishes spending time with her family. She is a dedicated wife and proud mother of two wonderful sons. Together with their beloved eight-year-old shichon, Snickers, the Trotman family resides in Ambler, Pennsylvania, where they enjoy the warmth and support of their close-knit community.

www.ingramcontent.com/pod-product-compliance
Lightning Source LLC
Chambersburg PA
CBHW031933190326
41519CB00007B/520